Your Nar

Rochelle Gordon is … metaphysics, a consultant and author of the popular 'What's in a Name?' column for *Horoscope* magazine. She appears on various radio and television talk shows and has lectured on the hermetic arts aboard the *QEII*.

Shirlee Kiley is a noted expert in the field of karmic astrology. She too has taught and lectured extensively and, as director of the Tenth House Center (an association that promotes psychic development), has conducted over eight hundred classes and workshops on astrology-related subjects.

Shirlee and Rochelle met through their memberships in the National Council for Geocosmic Research and the American Federation of Astrologers, and provide an acrophonological name evaluation and counseling service. For details, write to P.O. Box 173, West Nyack, New York 10994, or P.O. Box 1615, Cherry Hill, New Jersey 08034.

Shirlee Kiley
and Rochelle Gordon

Your Name Is Your Destiny

Pan Books London and Sydney

First published in Great Britain 1984 by Pan Books Ltd,
Cavaye Place, London SW10 9PG
This work is a revised and expanded version of
Please Don't Spell My Name Wrong
9 8 7 6 5 4 3 2 1

ISBN 0 330 28499 1
Printed and bound in Great Britain by
Hunt Barnard Printing Ltd, Aylesbury, Bucks.

DEDICATION

This book could not have been written without the support, love, and kindness of Milton and Sylvia Rubin, Cheryl Kiley, Clair and Mike Alpert, and the presence of Bennett Munch.

Contents

Preface

The Acrophonology knowledge you are about to learn will enable you to determine personality characteristics from a name, any name—even one that's yet to be given. You will be able to understand why certain names elicit certain emotional responses within you.

By using Acrophonology, you will be able to choose a name that fits your needs or has the qualities and characteristics you most desire. You can, in fact, apply what you are about to learn to improve your life. Every day we witness name changes that bring about life-style and energy changes or success to people such as movie stars, artists, and writers. We often feel the need for such a change to help accomplish a long-sought-after goal, but we do not know how to go about choosing a new name, or which expert to consult for help. Now you can be your own expert!

Acrophonology lets you discover your own energy patterns. This science will enable you to understand yourself and the energies of those around you.

1

The Science of Acrophonology

What's in a Name?

We are all called by some name. The vibratory qualities of sound affect our personality; the sounds of the letters in our name reflect our personality expressions. Each letter in the alphabet corresponds to a certain energy vibration that can be correlated to the signs of the zodiac. Your name can be interpreted in the same manner as your horoscope. Name evaluation in this form is done through the study known as Acrophonology.

The word "acrophonology" is derived from the Greek language and means the study of sound in space. Language is sound in space, and letters are symbols and energy activators for sounds. Sounds are energy vibrations. As energy, they affect our very being. Witness, for example, how the sounds emitted from the vocal cords of a trained singer can shatter a glass.

Acrophonology is an ancient science. It began as a study of letters found in the Kabbalah, which records the teachings of the ancient Hebrew mystics. The Kabbalah consists of five books, one of which, the Book of Numbers, instructs in the understanding of universal energies and incorporates Astrology, Numerology, and Acrophonology. This book holds knowledge of universal energies, which can aid man in his soul's travel and evolution.

The forms of these energies are constantly changing. A competent astrologer can interpret these energy changes by the movement of the celestial bodies: a numerologist through the numbers of each day, month, and year; and an acrophonologist through the letters in a person's name. The ancient science of Numerology also employs the use of letters. Pythagoras, the Greek philosopher and mathematician, assigned letter and astrological meanings to numbers. But Pythagoras was not the originator of this correlation. It was first introduced to esoteric students in the Kabbalah.

The letters in the name on your first documented birth record hold within them the energy patterns of your personality. The art/science of Astrology is based on the date, time, and place of birth. This maps the energy patterns that determine your life path, as heralded by your horoscope. These influences can also be noted from your numerology chart. Each of these cosmic blueprints—

Acrophonology, Astrology, and Numerology—provides information about you and how your personal energy pattern relates to the universal scheme of things.

According to mystical tradition, everything is named and numbered in the cosmos. You are your name!

A rose would still be a rose by any other name, 'tis true. But people are different. A George by any other name would not be the same man. Studies have been done to determine reactions to names. In July 1977, a *New York Times* survey revealed that a large percentage of teachers predetermined students' scholastic and mental abilities by their names. More recent studies by both British and American name societies have disclosed that your name influences your character and has a definite bearing on the path your life takes.

Names can also reflect social trends. The "flower children" of the 60s advocated love, not war. Their popular names sounded this note with use of the "**I** love you" letter **I** at the end of their names: Sandi, Jacki, Cindi, Jerri. The **I** energy is that of peace, involvement, and indulgence.

Where did all the **I**'s go? They are having children of their own now, and are naming them with these popular names taken from a list published in the March 1983 issue of *Parents Magazine*: Michael, Jason, Matthew, David, Brian, Christopher, Johnathan, John, James, Jeffrey, Jennifer, Ann, Jessica, Karen, Michelle, Katherine, Rebecca, Deborah, Robin, Megan. In fact, statistics proved that in 1982 there was a higher marriage rate and lower divorce rate than in the last decade. Many of these popular names begin with **D**, **M**, or **J**. The first letter of a given or first name carries the most weight in name evaluation and the strongest energy projection by the individual. The letters **D** and **M** symbolize motherhood and family energy flow. Societal movement is now turning back toward home and family values. The letter **J** speaks of international and foreign matters. This generation will bring forth a united world through expansion and interaction. They will be globetrotters with their roots firmly planted in patriotic home soil.

In the same way that popular names of a certain time period reflect trends in society, each individual's name spells out his or her own unique energy pattern. Energy manifests itself in many ways—physically, universally, mentally, emotionally, and spiritually. Physically, on a personal level, we experience energy as vitality and body awareness. Universally we experience energy as light, sound, and matter. Our feelings and physical sensations are an extension of our emotional energy flow. Mental energy is experienced through words, thoughts, and visualization. Spiritual energy is more refined and is acknowledged and received intuitively, or experienced on an inner plane of awareness. *There is order in the universe*.

Acrophonology enables you to better understand how these energy patterns affect you and those around you. You can now know the meaning of each letter in the alphabet as it corresponds to personality traits, characteristics, human desires, needs, and proclivities. For example, an individual whose name begins with the letter **S** is status conscious and strives for success. A person whose name begins with **D** is very home-oriented. Such an individual's main concern is his or her family life.

How do we know this?

How does Acrophonology work?

What is it based on?

Euclid wrote, "Things equal to the same thing are equal to each other." This is the axiom by which Acrophonology is understood. There is a correlation between the signs of the zodiac and the letters in the alphabet. For example, just as Aries people have leadership abilities, can be aggressive, get right in where the action is, and tend to be up-front, these very same qualities can be found in people whose names contain the letter **A**. Therefore, since the zodiacal sign Aries and the letter **A** carry the same energy value, they are one and the same thing. Each letter in the alphabet relates to an astrological sign, the meanings of which were described by the ancients centuries ago.

In the same way that the acorn holds within it the oak tree, the infant holds the full-grown adult. Each may be tempered in time, but the basic outcome is set in the beginning. And in the beginning each person is given a name that identifies the energies that he or she will embody. These energies can be individually defined through name evaluation.

Acrophonology was rediscovered and developed through years of research by the authors, who correlated horoscopes with names. Through this research, and in over ten thousand case studies, they discovered correspondences between astrological factors in birth charts and letters in birth names. In all cases, the correlations were provable and repeatable. As a result of their work, they've been able to establish a definable energy pattern for each letter of the alphabet. With the knowledge that they share, anyone can begin to unlock the secrets that lie hidden in a name and tap the power and energy that has been associated with names since the beginnings of mankind.

The importance of names has been known throughout the centuries. In many cultures two names are given to every newborn child. One is known only to close family members and the other is the commonly used name. This practice stems from the belief that there is power in a name. A name reveals both the strengths and weaknesses of the bearer.

Another example of the power to be gained by knowing a name can be found in the myth of the Egyptian goddess Isis. Legend says that Isis wanted to become an equal to the male sun god, Ra. She knew that the source of his power was held in his secret name and therefore arranged for him to be stung on the foot by a serpent. He called out for help. Isis offered to save him only if he disclosed his secret name, and Ra agreed. This is one explanation as to how Isis became an equal in power to Osiris.

In ancient Rome, before the advent of Christianity, a "name day" was held on the eighth day after birth for boys and on the ninth day for girls. A sacrifice was made in order to purify the name so that it could not be used as an incantation by a magician, who understood the power locked into the name.

Alfred Lord Tennyson, a poet and mystic, recorded in his diary his psychic experiences induced by repeatedly calling his name to get in touch with his higher self, as did all of the old mystics.

The Hawaiian kahunas of old—masters of religious and ceremonial lore—taught that to give something a name is to make it a complete thought form.

In India, the Vedas, or sacred Hindu writings, are recited by pundits, who by this recitation can know the form of the object through its name.

And finally, *The Book of the Bible* by Eunice Riedel, Thomas Tracy, and Barbara D. Moskowitz gives us further insights on the importance of names in biblical times. "In an astounding number of cases, children had names indicating the role they were to play in life, leading to the suspicion that they changed their names once their careers were launched or that biblical authors gave appropriate names to the people they wrote about."

Yes, there *is* power in a name, power that for centuries has been recognized and revered. This book will help you to understand and channel it.

2

You and Your Name

Your name as recorded at birth reveals your birthright and your genetic makeup. It spells out your individuality. It is the I.D. for your personality energies.

Just as no two people are exactly alike, there are truly no two names exactly alike either. The modifying factor is the mother's maiden name. Even though people may bear the same first, middle, and last names, only in the rarest of cases would their full name, including their mother's maiden name, be the same. American names do not always make use of the mother's maiden name, but in many nationalities—Hispanic and Chinese, for example—it is included in the individual's full name. Your mother's maiden name is a part of your heritage and a definite part of your energy flow. It is a key factor in interpreting your personality.

Astrologically, the time and location of birth is what gives each of us our own unique horoscope. Even twins born on the same day, in the same place, would not have been born at the exact same time. In addition, each twin is given his or her own first name. While the names may be similar, the spelling is different.

We do, however, know of a case in which twins were given the same first name. These twins are affectionately known as the "Jim twins." Dr. Thomas J. Bouchard of the University of Minnesota, who has conducted a study on identical twins reared apart, heard of this set of twins separated at birth and both named Jim by their adoptive families. They were reunited at age thirty-nine. Their lives are marked by astonishing similarities. Both had dogs named Toy, both married and divorced women named Linda and had second marriages to women named Betty; they named their sons James Allan and James Alan.

Appearing on the Phil Donahue television show in 1980, Dr. Bouchard described yet another set of separated twins in England who gave their children very similar names. One twin named her son and daughter Richard Andrew and Karen Louise. Her twin sister's children are named Andrew Richard and Katherine Louise, a surprising coincidence, to say the least, although Dr. Bouchard reminded his audience that naming is almost always the collaborative effort of both parents.

In the rare instances of astro twins—individuals with different parentage yet very close horoscopes—one would assume that the names would differ even though the charts are almost identical. However, we know of astro twins born 10 hours and 50 minutes apart, at the same longitude and extremely close latitudes (which gives them almost identical horoscopes), who have very similar names. One was born with a family name of Hendricks and the other, Hendrickson.

These few examples of the quirks of names and naming make one stop and think. How did the adoptive families of the "Jim twins" arrive at the same names? How does the idea of a name for a child enter a parent's mind? Does the child's soul or consciousness place it there? Are there psychic links between separated twins that cause them to name their children similarly? And what about the destinies of the children? How do the energy needs of the child's consciousness enter the picture? As it was so aptly put by Shakespeare's Hamlet, "There are more things in heaven and earth, Horatio, than are dreamt of in your philosophy."

The names that we use in our daily lives indicate the energies that are the most dominant and apparent in our everyday actions. We employ many types of energy patterns in any one day. We play many roles, which are reflected by our different names as well as by how we use those names. We often sign our names differently than we speak them. For instance, we may use just an initial rather than a full name when signing official or business documents. On the other hand, we may use our full name when signing personal letters or other types of correspondence. We sometimes use nicknames or abbreviated names. These name variations are indicative of our personality expressions and experiences at any given time. What we call ourselves signifies what we want to show the world. And, in turn, what we are called by others is a good indication of how they view us.

Each part of your full name has its own significance. In your mother's maiden name lies your lineage, your ancestral, family, and spiritual heritage, as well as your hidden karma, those subconscious motivations, talents, habits, and abilities of which you have no conscious awareness. The energy patterns found in this name will show the experiences and the personality needs and expressions of your mother during the time of your conception, gestation, and immediately following your birth. Some of these energy patterns are the product of her family upbringing and thus demonstrate inherited traits.

Your given name, first name, or nickname embodies the personality you present to others. It spells out your means of self-expression. It depicts how you relate to your environment, the people and circumstances that make up your world.

Your surname, or last name—whether it be a marriage or professional name—reveals what the world recognizes about you on an impersonal level. These names tell of your status, reputation, and the general formal presentation of your individuality.

The personality traits shown by your middle, second,

and/or confirmation names begin to take effect only between the ages of thirteen and fourteen, traditionally the age of coming into adulthood. If there is no such name, the mother's maiden name will take its place. This name shows energies you develop through experience and maturation, as well as acquired values that affect life choices.

Your name really is your calling card. It signifies energies you put forth consciously and subconsciously that may be perceived both by you and by others around you. The personality you reveal will determine the name you are called or that you call yourself. Each role played in life is reflected by the names used. You may be Mrs. Smith to a salesman and Mary to your friends. You exhibit different energies when you use different names, and each name calls forth a different energy response. Your various names define who you are. Let's now begin to learn how these definitions work—and how to make them work for you.

3

Rules for Name Evaluation

Each letter in the alphabet has its own meaning. These meanings are fully described in Chapter 4, where the dictionary provides definitions for each letter. It spells out what each letter means. You can put together a composite personality description by looking up the interpretation of each letter according to its position in a name.

In evaluating a name, it is important to be sure you are using the same spelling that the individual whose name you are evaluating uses, and not a commonly accepted version.

You can learn a great deal from one name. However, the more names available to you, the greater the insights you will discover about an individual's personality. For example, the surname will be more enlightening on a business level, whereas socially, it is the currently used first name that counts most.

For proper name evaluation, *all of a person's names must be used.* The name as documented on the first birth record is of paramount importance. Do not be misled by statements such as "I've never used the name on my birth certificate. I've always been called . . ." The birth record name still carries your energy identification and often discloses hidden tendencies. Confirmation names, nicknames, altered names, business, pen, or stage names, and initials must all be included for complete name evaluation. All and any of these names, even if not in current use, embody the energies that influence your character; therefore all of he names one carries must be evaluated. Appendages such as "Jr." and "III" do not count, as these are not considered names.

In the dictionary, you will find the following categories for each letter.

THRUST: The first letter of a name, excluding the surname category listed below.

KEY: The last letter of a name.

FIRST LETTER OF SURNAME: The first letter of the family name, last, marriage, or professional name used.

HINGE: The middle letter of a name, found only in names containing an odd number of letters.

RANDOM: All other letters in a name.

DOUBLE LETTER: The same letter placed together in a name—for example, **AA**, as in "**Aa**ron."

MULTIPLE LETTERS: The same letter found more than two times in a full name, whether placed together or not.

Acrophonology Worksheet

1. Mother's Maiden Name:

2. First Name Used:

3. Nickname Used:

4. First Name on Birth Certificate:

5. Middle Name on Birth Certificate:

6. Confirmation Name:

7. Other Name Used:

8. Surname on Birth Certificate:

9. Marriage Name:

10. Business Name:

Steps to Follow

1. First write down your full name, either on a separate sheet of paper or in the spaces provided on the Acrophonology Worksheet.
2. If you're using the worksheet and the name you're evaluating ends in a shaded box, the center letter is the hinge letter and the hinge letter and the name has an odd number of letters. If the name ends in an open box, there is no hinge letter and your name has an even number of letters.
3. Now divide the letters into two sections, as in the examples below. If the name ends in an open box, draw a line separating the letters evenly.

EXAMPLE

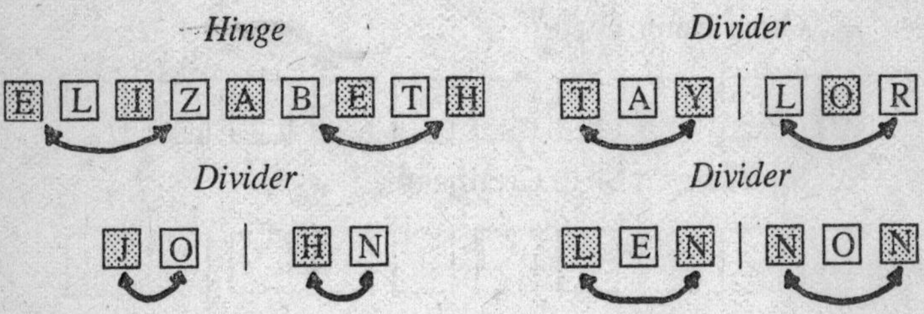

If you're not using the worksheet, you can simply count the letters in each name to determine if your first, middle, surname, and so on, have an even or odd number of letters. Remember to make these even-odd calculations separately, for each name.

EXAMPLE

ELIZABETH TAYLOR	JOHN LENNON
123456789 123456	1234 123456
(odd) (even)	*(even) (even)*

4. It should now be easy to identify the thrust, hinge, key, first letter of surname, random, double, and multiple letters for the names under evaluation. For instance, in the two examples given the thrust letters are **E** and **J**; the key letters are **H** and **R, N** and **N**; first letters of each surname are **T** and **L**; the hinge letter, which occurs only in ELIZABETH (because this is the only name above with an odd number of letters), is the middle letter, **A**. The random letters are **L, I, Z, A, B, E,** and **T** in ELIZABETH; **A, Y, L,** and **O** in TAYLOR, **O** and **H** in JOHN, and **E, N,** and **O** in LENNON. The double letters are **NN** in LENNON. There is only one multiple letter in the examples above—**N** in JOHN LENNON, as there are a total of four **N**'s, thus making more than two in the full name.
5. After you've determined the above letter information, turn to the dictionary where you'll find the energy

significances for each letter (depending on how they serve in a name, whether as thrust, hinge, key, random letter, and so on) spelled out in detail.

To give you an example of how to put the letter definitions together to arrive at a thorough evaluation of any full name, we've analyzed the names ELIZABETH TAYLOR and JOHN LENNON.

Evaluation of the Name ELIZABETH TAYLOR

ELIZABETH

E (Thrust): You have a need to communicate and express yourself, yet you may not always express yourself truly. You can easily overintellectualize and can't stand being misquoted. You require people around as you must have someone's ear. You have the gift of gab. A good many of your close relationships tend to be with individuals who are philosophical, adventurous, and bright.

L (Random): You are social and need contact with people. You wish to maintain peace and harmony in your environment. You have a diplomatic flair—relationships are a must for you. You believe that you know what's best for everyone and you don't mind telling them so, yet you can be refined, charming, and gracious. You can also be lethargic, indecisive, moody, intractable, and dogmatic.

I (Random): You enjoy the finer things in life, and you tend to expect things to come to you. And somehow things do effortlessly move in your direction. You have the ability to attract possessions and people. You share. You enjoy giving as well as receiving. You can be most affectionate, kind, and expressive of your love. Your nature is that of a peacemaker. You would rather make love than war. However, you are also pragmatic, practical, and sensible. You know that you need financial as well as emotional security. You will work for and go after what you want. Then there are the sensual, aesthetic, artistic, and earthy qualities deeply embedded in your nature. You are quite demonstrative in your show of affection.

Z (Random): You have intuitive abilities, are inwardly knowing and protected by higher forces. You can tap into these powers to gain the knowledge you seek. Fate may deal a dirty hand, but you are able to rise to the occasion. You are a private behind-the-scenes person, who can become a channel for helping others. But beware of allowing them to take advantage of you.

A (Hinge): You can be impatient and impetuous. You have difficulty dealing with authority. You try to beat the system before it beats you.

B (Random): Financial security is important to you. You tend to be fixed in your habits and thoughts. You enjoy luxuries, being catered to, taking it easy, and above all, expressing your sexuality. You are sensual and brainy at the same time. You may be passive, yet when aroused you are as strong as a bull and as sly as a fox. You can overcome all obstacles that stand in your way. You have inner determination and fortitude. You are a physical creature who desires comforts.

E (Random): You wish to exchange ideas. You have good verbal, expressive, and writing abilities. You relate well, are rational, logical, but can overintellectualize. You are clever, witty, and inventive, yet may be nervous and restless, easily scattering your thoughts. You are a storehouse of trivia.

T (Random): You are idealistic, intuitive, sensitive, skeptical and creative. You desire privacy. You seek knowledge of abstract truths, belief systems and principles, all of which operate within a universal framework. Your deep, compassionate feelings demonstrate themselves poetically. Your sensitive nature often gets the best of you, sometimes causing moodiness and depression. You seek answers. You have been known to be a Doubting Thomas.

H (Key): You tend to wrap things up by taking the most expedient course of action. Status and money are prominent factors in your life. You have a strong drive to earn, which can become a compulsion. Does the name Howard Hughes ring a bell? You are an eleventh-hour person who gets what you need in the nick of time. You desire quality as opposed to quantity. You feel you must achieve on your own. You have strong loner instincts. The close relationships that you do pursue tend to be with with individuals who depend on you and who let you tell them what to do. You enjoy being boss and running the show.

TAYLOR

T (Surname): You have an aptitude for helping those who cannot help themselves. You are creative; your artistic talents can be put to use in any field. Think, for example, of Tchaikovsky, Toulouse-Lautrec, Twinkle Toes, and Twain. Your visions and fantasies will come in handy for work in design, the media, and publicity. Travel intrigues you, which may lead you to international affairs . . . both business and personal. Your strong urge for freedom is paramount in your job selections. You need mental and emotional space, even if you cannot have actual physical space.

A (Random): You wish to be active and challenged, both mentally and physically, all the time. You have been known to turn others into nervous wrecks. You have an aptitude for problem solving, especially those problems you create yourself. You desire independence and want to be your own person. You can be assertive and aggressive, as well as brave and forthright. Your tendency is toward headstrong behavior, impatience, and innovative technique. You leap first and look later. Your enthusiasm can carry you away.

Y (Random): You seek out positions of authority, responsibility, status, and ways of achieving monetary success, all in an attempt to overcome deep feelings of insecurity. You must believe that you are in charge of your life. You are willing to work long and hard to achieve your goals. You can be disciplined, self-controlled, calculating, and frugal. You tend to put business before pleasure. You dislike taking orders. Independence is your personal byword.

L (Random): See above in Elizabeth.

O (Random): You are richly emotional and you try to channel your feelings into constructive uses. You have a highly developed sixth sense. When it comes to your loved ones, you are very loyal and protective. You have strong dependency needs, which you try to control. You have a tendency toward compulsive behavior. You are intense and put all of your energy into everything you do. You can be fixed in your opinions and slow to make changes. However, you are a powerhouse when set in motion.

R (Key): You tend to wrap things up by taking action only after careful consideration. You are self-reliant, outgoing, pioneering, innovative, and forward-thinking. You are willing to take actions and risks once you are set on a course. You have an active, logical, bright mind. You are determined and will fight for what you want. At times you have no patience and a low tolerance for nonsense and nonproductive activity. You weigh and balance all of your decisions. The strength of your mental abilities surfaces around age twenty-eight. You handle thoughts much better than emotions. Most of your close relationships tend to be with individuals who are social, intelligent, and attractive.

Evaluation of the Name JOHN LENNON

JOHN

J (Thrust): You have a love of sports, travel, and adventure. You have a strong sense of fair play, and need physical activity in order to stay healthy. You are moral and idealistic. You may carry out the letter of the law and sometimes lose sight of its intent. You set your goals very high. There is a strong sense of spirituality in your soul. You can be a perpetual student. You are creative and imaginative. Your close relationships tend to be with individuals who are interesting, diversified, and who talk a lot.

O (Random): See **O** in Taylor, above.

H (Random): You have a need to succeed in life. It is almost a compulsion. Achievement and self-attainment are primary driving forces. You measure your success by the amount of money and status you attain. Practicality, cunning calculations, and detached efficiency are your strong points. You can be shrewd, manipulating, conniving, and eclectic. You have a way of getting your heart's desire, no matter what that might be. You have much staying power as well as good business sense. Being independent and wealthy are virtues in your book.

N (Key): You wish to conclude matters in a conscientious, efficient manner. You have a need to be in control. That nice neat hypochondriacal nut of *The Odd Couple* fame reminds us of you. You are self-critical. You do not always express your own desires, sometimes putting the needs of others above your own. You get satisfaction out of working and doing a job well. You seek perfection in yourself and others, but may not admit this. You can be orderly, neat, exacting, self-disciplined, and a nit-picker. You have an interest in health matters. You want to feel needed. You worry too much. Your close relationships tend to be with individuals who let you do things for them.

LENNON

L (Surname): You have an aptitude for design, fashion, and public relations. Your diplomatic nature allows you to move in many diverse circles. You have a knack for the law and a strong sense of justice, like Sir Lancelot. You have speaking abilities as well as know-how when it comes to counseling and advising. You are happy when working with people, and will do well in partnerships.

E (Random): See **E** in Elizabeth, above.

N (Random): You are a hard worker when you get going. You think things through very carefully before deciding what to do or how to do it. You plan your strategy well. You have the ability to handle details. You can be quite health conscious, orderly, organized, exacting, and fussy. You can burden yourself with guilt. You take pride in a job well done. You want to help others and be of service. You are discerning, discriminating, and shy, even though you enjoy talking and socializing. (The letter **N** in this name has been analyzed as both a random and a double letter only for the purpose of illustration. Double letters need not be evaluated as random letters because the double letter energies are the dominant ones.)

NN (Double): You may be super-critical of yourself and others. You can go on health kicks or totally neglect your health. You are capable of holding down two jobs. You go to extremes, either being very industrious or very lazy—though most of the time it's industrious. It bothers you to leave something undone, so you will forgo leisure time to complete a task. You may find yourself leaning toward escapism, avoiding facing issues, and spending more time in your head than in reality. You may find yourself drawn to people who need your help. You do many tasks at once, not necessarily in any sequential order.

O (Random): See **O** in Taylor, above.

N (Multiple): You are efficient, can be a workaholic, and are very organized and overcritical.

4

Dictionary

This dictionary includes nine categories for each letter, as well as a general description of the energy patterns associated with them. (The **CH** combination has its own separate listing because it acts as one letter.) The categories are explained below.

SYNONYMS: These are words that begin with the letter or include it prominently. They capture the letter's energy expression. You can memorize each letter's synonym energy qualities and use this information to perform on-the-spot name analysis. They symbolize the force, power, and significance of the energy value of the letter.

DEFINITION: This provides a description of the character, flavor, power, and significance of the letter's energy flow. Both its positive and negative expressions are outlined. An individual with the defined letter in his or her name will on some level experience or demonstrate the types of energy depicted in the definition paragraph. The descriptions emphasize how the energies associated with the letter are manifested or become apparent in everyday life. *You will be able to recognize these energies in yourself and others.*

THRUST LETTER: This is the first letter of a name, except for surnames. (The first letter of a surname gets a category all to itself.) Because the thrust letter begins a name, it signifies the thrust of your personality expression. You lead and advance with these characteristics, wearing them on your sleeve, so to speak. The traits described for this letter, and the key letter, are the strongest personality qualities of all in name evaluation.

One further note on thrust letter definitions: The personality traits demonstrated in this letter position are so strong that they can generally also be applied when interpreting the significance of key letters and first letters of surnames. Therefore, it's wise to check thrust definitions as well when evaluating the key and first letter of a surname position.

KEY LETTER: This is the last letter of a name. As this closes off a name, the traits described for this letter will indicate how you conclude things. We enter with the thrust letter personality qualities and leave via key letter traits. *The characteristics defined for the key letter, along with* *those of the thrust letter, should receive the greatest emphasis in your evaluation of a name.*

FIRST LETTER OF SURNAME, (Including family name, and last, marriage, or professional name): These names indicate the energies that the world recognizes about you on an impersonal level. They tell of your status, reputation, and your overall formal presentation out of the home. The first letter of this name gives clues as to your career goals. It is the energy you lead with in presenting your formal self, in putting your best foot forward in social situations. In this regard, it carries the same amount of energy clout as the thrust and key letters. It is a good idea to always refer to the thrust and key letter descriptions as well in analyzing the significance of this letter.

HINGE LETTER: This is the middle letter of a name. It is found only in names containing an odd number of letters. Hinge letter energies are blocked: therefore, they do not flow freely. They are either held in and make themselves felt in subconscious or disguised forms, or they push so hard to come out that they become out of synch, exaggerated and abrasive. Hinge letter energies are usually experienced as obsessions, compulsions, and blocks, which are overcome, or should be overcome, for personality growth.

RANDOM LETTER: This letter can be found anywhere in a name, except for the first and last positions.

DOUBLE LETTER: The same letter placed together, side by side, such as **AA**. These energies have a double whammy effect, can be experienced as dualism and behavior exhibiting both sides of a coin with extremes drawn from either end of the energy spectrum.

MULTIPLE LETTERS: The same letter found more than twice in the full name, whether or not any of the letters are placed together. This gives added emphasis to the energies of this letter in the personality expression.

Keywords

You might wish to memorize the keywords for each letter listed below. That way, when you meet someone, you can make a quick assessment of his or her personality. For example, while an acquaintance tells you how laid-back he or she is, you can note that his or her name begins with **CH**, revealing an energy flow that requires change and challenge. This person could not possibly remain laid-back for long. You can use each keyword for your own information or to dazzle others with your insights.

Also listed below are the zodiacal signs for each letter. If you have an understanding of the signs, this will give you an even greater sense of the qualities found in the letter.

LETTER	KEYWORD	ZODIACAL SIGN
A	Action	Aries
B	Beauty	Taurus
B	Brains	Libra
C	Curious	Gemini

CH	Change	Scorpio
CH	Challenge	Capricorn
D	Domestic	Cancer
E	Expressive	Gemini
F	Friendly	Leo
G	Gregarious	Gemini
G	Go-getter	Virgo
H	Heart's Desire	Capricorn
H	Hope	Aquarius
I	I love you	Taurus
J	Justice	Sagittarius
J	Joy	Pisces
K	Kundalini (*Hindu, for power*)	Scorpio
L	Lover	Taurus
L	Logical	Libra
M	Mother	Cancer
N	Neat	Virgo
O	Obstinate	Cancer
O	Obsessive	Scorpio
P	Pretty	Taurus
P	Pensive	Libra
Q	Quick	Sagittarius
R	Reason	Aries
S	Success	Capricorn
T	Truth	Sagittarius
T	Doubting Thomas	Pisces
U	Understanding	Sagittarius
U	Universality	Pisces
V	Variety	Aquarius

W	Willful	Leo
X	Excited	Gemini
Y	Yin/Yang	Capricorn
Z	Zigzag	Pisces

A

SYNONYMS: Action, Assertive, Aggressive, Ambitious, Argumentative, Angry.

DEFINITION: This is an active energy that must flow in an outgoing manner. Once the flow begins, there is no stopping it. Positively it can be experienced as assertiveness, ambition, drive, bravery, leadership, independence, forthrightness, and as a pioneering spirit. Negatively it can be experienced as forcefulness, impatience, rudeness, crudeness, pushiness, and bossiness.

THRUST LETTER: You have definite leadership abilities that you don't always exercise. You have a tendency to assert yourself, but this is usually done in a diplomatic manner. You are adventurous, but can be foolhardy, especially when carried away by your own enthusiasm. Establishing a self-identity through your own actions is of paramount importance to you. You are headstrong. Your physical needs are of primary concern. Above all, you must do your own thing! Your close relationships tend to be with individuals who are peace-loving, cooperative, and sociable. . . . You know, the types you can push around.

KEY LETTER: You tend to wrap things up through

independent action and you never look back. (See thrust letter description.)

FIRST LETTER OF SURNAME: You have an aptitude for problem solving. You handle crises well. You are ambitious and strive toward success. You require a challenge in your work. You are a go-getter, working best on your own. Boredom is your curse. Your talents lie in being an entrepreneur. You can start at the bottom and rise to the top in a short period of time.If you don't get there fast enough, you will just step on a few heads. You need to exercise your initiative and creativity. You will be happiest being your own boss. (See thrust letter description.)

HINGE LETTER: You can be impatient and impetuous. You have difficulty dealing with authority. You try to beat the system before it beats you.

RANDOM LETTER: You wish to be active and challenged, both mentally and physically, all the time. You have been known to turn others into nervous wrecks. You have an aptitude for problem solving, especially those you create yourself. You want your independence and desire to be your own person. You can be assertive and aggressive, as well as brave and forthright. Your tendency is toward headstrong behavior, impatience, and innovative techniques. You leap first and look later. Your enthusiasm can carry you away.

DOUBLE LETTER(AA): You may exhibit passive-aggressive behavior: "I'll go to any movie you choose, but it has to be one I like." You especially pull these little numbers in personal relationships. Your tendency will be to avoid conflict; however, if pushed too far, you will fight and never let your partner hear the end of it. You may notice you can go from valor to foolhardiness. You can be impatient, optimistic, excitable, headstrong, quick to make judgments, and impulsive; yet at other times, ambivalent, unable to make decisions or take action, holding back due to fear. Your temper flares. You have two distinct levels of personality. One minute you are peace-loving; the next, a battering ram.

MULTIPLE LETTERS: You have high aspirations and desire to better yourself. You seem to require challenge and crisis in your life, which you can subconsciously draw to yourself, or which may appear to come to you through others. Douglas MacArthur often wondered how he got himself into such a messy predicament.

B

SYNONYMS: Beauty, Brains, Bountiful, Bashful.

DEFINITION: This is a building energy that must flow through creative channels and attain tangible results. Positively it can be experienced as appreciation of beauty, luxury, the creature comforts, and the finer things in life. There is a strong money orientation to this letter and a need for financial security. This energy can be aesthetic, solid, persevering, and determined. It is practical, down-to-earth, pragmatic, pleasure-seeking, and peace-loving. It is constructive, resourceful, and has the ability to attract to it what it wants. Negatively it can be experienced as vanity, hoarding, possessiveness, extreme materialism, laziness, stubbornness, false pride, as well as overstimulation and gratification of the senses.

THRUST LETTER: You enjoy beauty and have a highly developed aesthetic sense. You love the material comforts of life, and are highly sentimental. You find it hard to throw anything away, from old shoes, to old pictures, to old lovers. . . . You need to feel appreciated. You require demonstrative love and affection: "Show me. Don't tell me." You are a physically sensual being and need to be stroked. You are strong-willed and can be opinionated. You take pride in your physical appearance. You and **B**urt Reynolds have much in common. As a rule, you are good-looking; take **B**o Derek, for example. You need to feel loved, even worshipped. You seek out individuals with status and brains, as you value these qualities in people. Basically, you are a snob.

KEY LETTER: Your creature comforts are most important. Financial security is paramount and you have a special penchant for stocks, bonds, and gold bullion. (See also thrust letter description.)

FIRST LETTER OF SURNAME: You have an aptitude for a career in finance or in a field dealing with luxury items. You have financial acumen and can handle other people's money. You are a good judge of quality, you know the value of a dollar, and your talents lie in being practical, persevering, and determined. You will work hard so that you do not have to work. At heart, you love to laze around and enjoy a life of leisure. (See thrust letter description.)

HINGE LETTER: You have to develop a sense of self-worth. You often seek stimulation of the senses, for example, by making mad passionate love or by eating. You can have a compulsive personality.

RANDOM LETTER: Financial security is important to you. You tend to be fixed in your habits and thoughts. You enjoy luxuries, being catered to, being lazy, and, above all, expressing your sexuality. You are sensual and brainy at the same time. You may be passive, yet when aroused you are as strong as a bull and as sly as a fox. You can overcome all obstacles that stand in your way. You have inner determination and fortitude. You are a physical creature desiring physical comforts.

DOUBLE LETTER(BB): You must learn to let go of old emotions, habits, and ideas. You may find that instead of fulfilling your secret desire to laze around, you are driven to accomplish and achieve. You can be torn between self-indulgence and austerity. There can be a compulsion to rid yourself of unwanted or undesirable character traits. You are practical, peace-loving, passive, and hardheaded. You have a double set of values and hidden assets.

MULTIPLE LETTERS: You have a constructive mind, a good memory, and the ability to handle money. You wish to acquire money so that you can enjoy the things that only it can buy. You have a sensual nature, which you can indulge lavishly on a regular basis. You prefer quality to quantity.

C

SYNONYMS: Curious, Clever, Cute, Chatty, Choice, Copycat, Candid.

DEFINITION: This is a mental as well as a social energy. Ideas must be shared and expressed. The mind must be used and developed. It can be experienced positively as cleverness, inventiveness, adaptability, youthfulness, mimicry, creativity, imaginative abilities, talent, wittiness, and sharp, clever thinking. It can be experienced negatively as nervousness, restlessness, the "curiosity that killed the cat," gossiping, deceit, stretching the truth, and trickery.

THRUST LETTER: You are a creative individual, not necessarily artistic, but ingenious and talented in many ways. You learn very quickly, often by just listening and watching. You extrapolate upon what you have observed. You want to know everything, and sometimes think you do. You enjoy pretending, acting, wearing costumes, talking, and creating an image. The name Cassius Clay comes to mind here. You are a chameleon, adopting the philosophies of those with whom you are involved. You will always remain youthful. Many of your close relationships tend to be with individuals who are philosophical, outdoorsy, fair-minded, with sharp intellects . . . and who can sometimes be stuffed shirts, opinionated, and sarcastic comics.

KEY LETTER: You rely heavily upon logic and reason. You can overintellectualize and may try to find answers to fit all circumstances, even when none is required. (See thrust letter description.)

FIRST LETTER OF SURNAME: You have an aptitude for teaching, selling, inventing, and working in any field that deals in communications. You have an active mind that must be challenged constantly. Anything that becomes routine will interfere with your attitude and your job performance. You have writing and speaking abilities. You are a people-person who enjoys making contacts. You are a great agent, go-between, and matchmaker. You will be happy in a career that allows for the use of your creative, imaginative, and mental abilities. Clarabelle the Clown and Inspector Clouseau have nothing on you. (See thrust letter description.)

HINGE LETTER: You need to learn concentration and to avoid scattering your energies. Don't try to do everything in one lifetime! You can learn to skydive next time around.

RANDOM LETTER: You must exercise your brain, your communicative and expressive abilities. You are aware of your environment and the people who surround you. You may keep your sharp observational abilities hidden from others. You enjoy interacting with all kinds of people. You can be quite clever and witty, but sometimes you talk too much.

DOUBLE LETTER(CC): You learn easily and have a desire for knowledge. Really, you want to know everything, and you may never stick to one subject. You can get into too many things at once and thereby run into confusion and lack of direction. You are chitchatty, a quality that makes you a good teacher and lecturer. You can be philosophical and moralistic, yet at the same time, quite adventurous and very easily bored. Your tendency to overextend yourself brings difficulties in attaining goals. Also, some of your goals may be too high or unrealistic.

MULTIPLE LETTERS: You are a highly creative person, as well as a blabbermouth.

CH

SYNONYMS: **Ch**ange, **Ch**allenge, **Ch**arge (as in **ch**arge account), **Ch**eck (as in **ch**ecking account).

DEFINITION: This is an energy that requires purpose, direction, regeneration, transformation, and growth, as well as success. It can be experienced positively as determination, perseverence, the surmounting of great obstacles, intensity, deep psychological insight, astuteness, good financial and business sense, and savvy. It can be experienced negatively as inertia, stagnation, pollution, insecurity, jealousy, possessiveness, and miserliness.

THRUST LETTER: You are a serious-minded individual who strongly wishes to succeed in life and who can survive by wits alone. You are street-wise, just like **Ch**arlie the Tuna. The promise of luck, health and a long life is yours for the asking. Many of your close relationships tend to be with individuals who are supportive of your career needs, who are bright, and who provide you with emotional stimulation . . . and let's not forget physical stimulation, as well. You are a pretty sexy character. Is your name **Charo**?

You have affinities with the characteristics found under the thrust letter **C.**

KEY LETTER: You tend to wrap things up in an efficient, tight, and very final manner. Your determination to persevere against all odds sets an example for others, also making you look like a stubborn ox. You have the ability to transform yourself, to rise like a phoenix from the ashes of your old self to a greater height than you ever thought possible. When asked how you managed this feat, you can't answer. Dumb luck! This is so. **CH** at the end of a name brings luck and ultimate financial success.

FIRST LETTER OF SURNAME: You have an aptitude for monetary matters, night work, and sneaking about like **Ch**arlie **Ch**an. You will be happy in a line of work that provides a challenge and affords you status. You have a tendency to change careers.

HINGE LETTER as in (Ri**ch**ie): You have a strong need to upgrade your life on a regular basis, like starting all over just as you have reached the top, or quitting your job just before you're due for a vacation. You must transform, purge, and regenerate regularly.

RANDOM LETTER: You are ever ready for a challenge. Personal priorities will change toward midlife. You take life seriously, often too seriously. You are a no-nonsense person. You are responsible, trustworthy, money- and status-oriented. You will surmount any obstacle placed in your path. Your middle name is Superman. At times, you can be jealous, insecure, miserly, and possessive. But no matter what it takes, you *will* transform your negatives into positives

TWO OR MORE CH COMBINATIONS: You have a compulsive personality. Your motto is all or nothing at all.

D

SYNONYMS: **D**omestic, **D**utiful, **D**a**dd**y, **D**oting, **D**emanding, **D**etermined.

DEFINITION: This is a determined, nurturing, emotional energy that must have a sense of being needed, cared for and/or caring for. It is a child looking for a parent and a parent looking for a child. Family ties are important—ties, not knots. It can be experienced positively as receptiveness, family closeness, sympathy, loyalty, shrewdness, resourcefulness, and tenacity. Negatively it can be experienced as clinging, moody, childish behavior, crybaby overdependency, as well as protectiveness to the point of possessive love, excessive shyness, and stubbornness.

THRUST LETTER: Your world, good or bad, revolves around your family. You wish to remain in the protective environment of a family, even an extended family, like a commune or harem. You hold your feelings inside. You are strongly nurturant, traditional, and patriotic. You, like the Boy Scouts, are trustworthy, loyal, helpful, friendly, courteous, kind, obedient, cheerful, thrifty, brave, clean, and reverent. You do your good deeds daily (like helping little old ladies across the street) and have a burning desire to help, even if help is not requested. You *know* what is best for all concerned. Your word is your bond, even if foolishly given. Many of your close relationships tend to be with individuals who are stable.

KEY LETTER: You are always helpful, protective, and emotionally involved in matters, good and bad. (See thrust letter description.)

FIRST LETTER OF SURNAME: You have an aptitude for professions that take care of the needs of people. You can work in the food, clothing, or shelter industries. You can also work with children. This may be in a day-care setting, teaching, or perhaps health care for families. You have an aptitude for money management and may be involved in the financial end of these fields. As you are sincere, you will find others coming to you with their problems. You are a do-gooder by nature. You will be happy working with and for the public. For example, watch Phil Donahue and John Denver, in action. (See thrust letter description.)

HINGE LETTER: You have a need to properly evaluate family bonds. You may have very strong ties to Mommy and Daddy. You must handle your feelings, and avoid allowing them to handle you.

RANDOM LETTER: You must know you are loved and protected at all times. Family life is important. You enjoy solving other people's problems. You can be tenacious, loyal, persevering, determined, shrewd, stubborn, and moody. You like playing a parent role. You must guard against your "children" becoming too dependent or demanding. You have a kind, loving, caring, emotional nature. You enjoy watching growth: You can overwater your plants and stuff your pets with too many choice morsels.

DOUBLE LETTER(DD): You feel you must establish financial security for yourself and family. You strive to protect the family name and position. You are a collector of "things." Your emotions can sometimes get in your way, and you need to learn to handle them. You wish to be the protector and at the same time the protected.

MULTIPLE LETTERS: You have a great deal of family pride, as well as a discriminating and overly emotional nature. You are a collector of valuables and a sentimentalist.

E

SYNONYMS: Expressive, Entertain, Environment, Exaggerate, Enlighten, Enliven.

DEFINITION: This is an energy that requires the use and expression of the intellect, the development of the mind and the thinking as well as the communicative processes. It must relate and connect to what is happening in the environment . . . like the neighborhood *yenta*. It can be experienced positively as verbalization and socialization. Writing, speaking, and teaching skills are evident, as well as inquisitiveness, creativity, wit, and dexterity. Negatively this energy can be experienced as nosiness, nervousness, restlessness, and nonstop talking that might well earn you the nickname of "motor-mouth"; other negative expressions of the Energy include overintellectualization, exaggeration, deception, and confusion.

THRUST LETTER: You have a need to communicate and express yourself, yet you may not always express yourself truly. You can easily overintellectualize and you can't stand being misquoted. You require people around as you must have someone's ear. You have the gift of gab. A good many of your close relationships tend to be with individuals who are philosophical, adventurous, and bright.

KEY LETTER: You tend to talk things out, sometimes to excess, and you employ reason, logic, and rational explanations. (See thrust letter description.)

FIRST LETTER OF SURNAME: You have an aptitude for selling, communicating, and teaching. Your mind is constantly on overtime. Thoughts never stop, especially creative ones. You are always one step ahead of yourself and everyone else. You can entertain, amuse, and enlighten. You are a connector, a go-between, an agent. You bring people together. You will be happy with a job that lets you travel and talk: politician, performer, or con man. (See thrust letter description.)

HINGE LETTER: You can talk endlessly, without ever saying what you *really* mean. You stretch the truth at times.

RANDOM LETTER: You wish to exchange ideas. You have good verbal, expressive, and writing abilities. You relate well, are rational and logical, but can overintellectualize. You are clever, witty, and inventive, yet you may be nervous and restless, easily scattering your thoughts. You are a storehouse of trivia.

DOUBLE LETTER(EE): You have much curiosity and the ability to learn rapidly. You can bluff your way through any subject. You are a fast talker. You can deal well in mental and communication areas, such as learning, teaching, selling, advertising, and writing. You are inventive, dexterous, witty, sly, clever, and a blabbermouth.

MULTIPLE LETTERS: You are quite talkative and inquisitive. You want to know everything. You always read more than one book at a time.

F

SYNONYMS: **F**riendly, **F**estive, **F**iery, **F**un-loving.

DEFINITION: This is an energy of love, joy, happiness, ego expression, and fulfillment. It has a need to shine, to take the stage and get feedback from others. It is creative. It can be experienced positively as leadership and executive abilities. **F** people have a talent for bringing joy and happiness to others. They exhibit generosity; a warm, loving heart; a fun-loving nature; and a fondness for children. It is optimistic, romantic, and dramatic energy. It provides a happy-go-lucky disposition. It can be experienced negatively as selfishness, egotism, snobbishness, a quickness to make judgments, prejudice, and an unforgiving heart. It can also express itself in false pride and isolation tendencies.

THRUST LETTER: You have a need to express yourself

creatively, as well as to feel loved and appreciated. You require lots of attention and like to fly high. You can be warm and kindhearted and very generous. You are exceptionally friendly but tend to avoid intimate contacts. You feel more secure in group endeavors than on a one-to-one basis. You have a need to be liked by everyone. A good many of your close relationships tend to be with individuals who are independent, standoffish, and unique in some way.

KEY LETTER: You tend to wrap things up by taking charge. (See thrust letter description.)

FIRST LETTER OF SURNAME: You can deal well with the public. You have leadership abilities. You may do well in the entertainment field or the political arena. You are dramatic and draw attention to yourself, just like Frances Farmer. You take pride in your career. It is a matter of ego for you to do well and attain respect and appreciation for your work. However, if you feel your efforts are being ignored, you may become quite unhappy, internalizing your dissatisfaction and feeling rejected. A creative career will keep you most happy, like Dr. Frankenstein's, for example. (See thrust letter description.)

HINGE LETTER: You have a need to learn the true meaning of friendship. You need attention and you may find yourself doing anything to be on center stage.

RANDOM LETTER: You have a need to shine and feel appreciated for who you are, not what you do. You are fun-loving, generous, and warm. However, there are times when you can be selfish, snobbish, egotistical, and judgmental. You are a proud person who is most happy when sharing good times with friends. You can be quite romantic and idealistic. You are a leader with a knack for bringing out flair and pizzazz in others.

DOUBLE LETTER(FF): You are extremely friendly. You come on strong, then back off, fearing you have gotten too close. You have strong ego needs, are highly sensitive and easily hurt. You have a need for an audience, even if you make a fool of yourself to get one. You enjoy being with people. It seems at times as if you can never get enough attention and expressions of love from those around you.

MULTIPLE LETTERS: You are extremely friendly and enjoy being with people, as well as being the center of attention.

G

SYNONYMS: Gregarious, Go-getter, Goof-off, Genuine.

DEFINITION: This is an energy of hard work where neatness counts. A strong work ethic and being of service is important. Awareness of health matters is evident. The sound working order of the body is necessary for you to achieve peace of mind. Positively this energy is experienced as hard work; efficiency; logical, rational thinking; orderliness; and a highly developed conscience with a good deal of guilt to accompany it. Negatively it can be experienced as a restlessness and being a workaholic or a professional loafer, a nervous talker, a hypochondriac, a fusspot, and picky, picky, picky.

THRUST LETTER: You enjoy a job done well. You have high standards and tend to require the same of others. (You are no fun to work with.) You are either very diligent or very lazy, and generally a combination of both. You lean toward procrastination; however, if you are in the right mood, no one can get the job done better than you. You strive for perfection and worry when things do not turn out just so. You talk a lot and you think a lot, getting caught up in details. You have a dry sense of humor. A good many of your close friends are people who are intuitive, sensitive, spacey, and creatively inclined. They are always trying to let you take care of things.

KEY LETTER: You tend to wrap things up efficiently, succinctly, and quite matter-of-factly. (See thrust letter description.)

FIRST LETTER OF SURNAME: You have an aptitude for work that is detailed and requires concentration. You are efficient, diligent, and a sought-after employee. You enjoy doing a job well. You switch from being a compulsive worker to an idle loafer. You go to extremes. You are happy when perfecting your skills, as well as goofing off. (See thrust letter description.)

HINGE LETTER: You have a need to properly evaluate how you do work and to give service. You can overdo, push too hard, and give too much. You can go from one end of the energy spectrum to the other, either being a workaholic or a professional loafer.

RANDOM LETTER: You want to know all the facts in all situations. Some folks might call you nosy. Being around people is important, as you enjoy helping them. You may be mentally compartmentalized and critical and are definitely conscientious, especially when it comes to work and health matters. You're a worrier and a perfectionist. You relate well to the Felix Unger half of *The Odd Couple*. Your hidden Oscar Madison double is gregarious, friendly, and puts worries and work aside—but not for too long. Your go-getter Felix side spars with your goof-off Oscar inclinations.

DOUBLE LETTER (GG): You feel strong obligations to take on the responsibilities of others, even when it is none of your business. You play the martyr role well. You tend to vacillate between being very fastidious and very sloppy. Your tendency is to be analytical, critical, discerning, shy, yet talkative, charming, and a marvelous host.

MULTIPLE LETTERS: You take pride in your work, in your health, and in your logical mind.

H

SYNONYMS: **H**eart's Desire, **H**ope, **H**yper, **H**obnobbing, **H**aggle.

DEFINITION: This is an energy that seeks success, status, and monetary gains, and it will take on challenge and responsibility to attain them. This energy can be experienced positively as being shrewd, eclectic, forward-thinking, group-oriented, and on the move. It is serious, has good business sense and staying power. It can be experienced negatively as rebelliousness, selfishness, miserliness, strictness, worry, insecurity, loneliness, and the avoidance of responsibility.

THRUST LETTER: Status and money are prominent factors in your life. You have a strong drive to earn, which can become a compulsion. Does the name **Howard Hughes** ring a bell? You are an eleventh-hour person, always getting what you need in the nick of time. You desire quality as opposed to quantity. You feel you must achieve on your own. You have strong loner instincts. The close relationships that you do have tend to be with individuals who depend on you and who let you tell them what to do. You enjoy being boss and running the show.

KEY LETTER: You always look for the most expedient course of action. (See thrust letter description.)

FIRST LETTER OF SURNAME: You are a leader and have managerial abilities. You wish to rise to a position of prominence in your career. You like to think of yourself as a forward-thinking humanitarian. You're geared to work that helps others as well as provides you with monetary remuneration. You are a good planner and organizer. You seek status and recognition, and have excellent business sense. You prefer to be your own boss, and you're happiest when in charge and acting upon your innovative, far-reaching ideas, which most people don't appreciate. When you make up your mind to move ahead, there is nothing that can stop you. Hedda Hopper knew all about that. (See thrust letter description.)

HINGE LETTER: You must learn to assess the true value of material possessions and to handle responsibility.

RANDOM LETTER: You have a compulsion to succeed in life. Achievement and attainment are primary, driving forces. You measure your success by the amount of money and status you have. Practicality, cunning calculations, and detached efficiency are your strong points. You can be shrewd, manipulating, conniving, and eclectic. You have a way of getting your heart's desire, no matter what that might be. You have staying power as well as business sense. Independence and wealth are virtues in your book.

DOUBLE LETTER(HH): Material success and status are high priorities in your life. Once you get it, you flaunt it. You are a take-charge person and have trouble allowing others to do for you. Although you are family-oriented, you can have problems dealing with the demands of family life. Business before pleasure. You are independent, individualistic, and reserved, tending to mind your own business and go it alone.

MULTIPLE LETTERS: You will always get your heart's desire and should never be broke. You are status conscious.

I

SYNONYMS: I love you, Intimate, Indulgence, Involved.

DEFINITION: This is an energy of love given and love

received. It is sensual, earthy, and needs to be appreciated for its beauty and charm. It is realistic, practical, and money-oriented. Positively it can be experienced as a kind, caring, warm, loving, sensual nature. There is a fine appreciation of the arts, fashion, things of luxury and comfort, as well as a highly developed sense of aesthetics, peace, and harmony. This energy can be experienced negatively as stinginess, subbornness, possessiveness, overindulgence, and a loss of values. The value loss can especially be noted in the game of people versus possessions. Also coming into play with this letter is false pride and overgratification and stimulation of the senses.

THRUST: You take pride in your physical appearance. You are a true, loyal friend. You desire to demonstrate your love and affection. You enjoy receiving attention. You take pleasure in your sensual nature. You want others to love you unconditionally and tend to test their love and martyr yourself in the name of love. You are inclined toward laziness. Your close relationships seem to be with individuals who are serious, intense, and deep thinkers.

KEY LETTER: You want to wrap things up in a practical, realistic manner that maintains the status quo. You have difficulty adjusting to change. You make sensuousness into a high art form. (See thrust letter description.)

FIRST LETTER OF SURNAME: You have an aptitude for creative work and will not readily give in to defeat. You like to build a solid foundation and structure in your work. You have an aptitude for a career in a financial field or in a field dealing in luxury items, works of art, and beauty.

You must see the tangible results of your labor. Most of all, you will be very happy when earning lots of money.

HINGE LETTER: You have a need to learn to give and receive love, simply for love's sake. You also have a need to be assured of affection.

RANDOM LETTER: You enjoy the finer things in life. Some might call you lazy, as you tend to expect things to come your way; and somehow things do. You have the ability to attract possessions and people. You share, and take joy in giving as well as receiving. You can be most affectionate, kind, and expressive. Your nature is that of a peacemaker—you would rather make love than war. However, you are also pragmatic, practical, and sensible. Knowing that you need both financial and emotional security, you will work for and go after what you want. There are, as well, sensual, aesthetic, artistic, and earthy qualities deeply embedded in your nature. You are very demonstrative in your show of affection.

DOUBLE LETTER(II): You have a deep need to give and receive love, and you go through turmoil if you suspect you're not giving enough love, easily falling into the martyr role. You don't want to gamble with your affections, and you first must be assured you will not be rejected before demonstrating your love. You are self-disciplined, often driving yourself hard to get what you want, which usually means financial and material attainments. You have a private, almost secret side to your nature. You need to feel monetarily secure, as well as attractive to a love partner. You are sensual, lazy, a comfort-lover, as well as determined and stubborn.

MULTIPLE LETTERS: You require an active, demonstrative love life and need to feel attractive to your partner. You must feel monetarily secure. You are very sensual and quite often involved with more than one person at one time.

J

SYNONYMS: Justice, Joy, Journey, Journal, Jester, Judicial.

DEFINITION: This is an energy of mental and spiritual expansion and growth, constantly seeking new horizons and new awareness. This energy can be experienced positively as being just and fair, and can include open-minded religious, spiritual, and philosophical exploration. You enjoy sports, travel, and all things foreign. This energy causes you to aspire to great heights. (We said aspire, not necessarily *attain* those great heights.) It brings a highly developed imagination. Negatively this energy can be experienced as excitability, a short attention span, sarcasm, a judgmental or bigoted nature, tactlessness, prejudice, and self-righteousness.

THRUST LETTER: You have a love of sports, travel, and adventure. Just call you James Bond or "007" for short. You have a strong sense of fair play, which you carry into your enthusiasm for sports. You have a need for physical activity; in fact, your body almost demands it. You are moral and idealistic to an extreme and may carry out the letter of the law while losing sight of its intent. You set your goals very high, sometimes unrealistically high. There is a strong sense of spirituality in your soul. You could be a perpetual student. You are creative and imaginative. Your close relationships tend to be with individuals who are interesting, diversified, and talkative.

KEY LETTER: You try to end matters by doing what you believe is correct, moral, or a terrific idea even if it is not feasible. Nothing stops you! (See thrust letter description.)

FIRST LETTER OF SURNAME: You have an aptitude for foreign affairs, publishing, and writing. You can become involved in the import/export business or the travel industry. Your philosophical leanings can lead you to education, teaching, and travel for personal enrichment. You can work in the courts as well as any other law-related pursuit. Your sports orientation opens many career doors. You have vision and the ability to know what the public wants. Your creative talents can be used in the advertising field. You will be happy in a career that challenges your intellect and allows you to put your beliefs into practice. (See thrust letter description.)

HINGE LETTER: You have a need to learn discrimination, justice, and fairness. You may try to avoid reality.

RANDOM LETTER: You have a need to explore, search out, and investigate all matters beyond your grasp. You look for understanding, knowledge, and explanations. You are excitable, enthusiastic, idealistic, future-oriented, and sometimes sarcastic. You are a just, fair person, who is also optimistic and expansive. You can be tactless and bold. You get bored very easily, and derive satisfaction from physical activity. You love to travel and to learn. Your mind is always racing and your curiosity knows no bounds.

DOUBLE LETTER(JJ): You have a strong sense of morals and can sometimes be fanatical in your beliefs. Your passion for justice can easily create a sense of frustration as you find that others do not always share your views. There are times when you can be scattered, absentminded, noncommittal, and fickle. You have been known to have a double set of standards; nevertheless, you always think *big*. You are abundantly optimistic and enthusiastic, though prone to exaggerate. You are a skeptic, as well as the proverbial **J**ack-of-all-trades and master of none.

MULTIPLE LETTERS: You can be highly spiritual or religious. Your sense of fair play and justice can overtake much of your thinking. You can be a sports nut.

K

SYNONYMS: **K**undalini, **K**arate, **K**arma, **K**ind.

DEFINITION: This is an energy of power. The Hindus call it Kundalini, also known as the creative force. It is generated in man through his gonads. This force is silent, effective, and deadly. It is so powerful that it not only creates life, but takes it away. It is to be treated with respect. It can be experienced positively as psychological insight and familiarity with the workings of the psyche. It bestows physical strength (King Kong), as well as mental and emotional strength. It is transformative (Helen Keller). There is a need for change and renewal, which is ongoing throughout life. There is depth to the energies of this letter, intensity, control, and willpower. It provides a knack for handling other people's money and promises a relatively long life. **K** energy can be experienced negatively as extreme secretiveness, possessiveness, jealousy, lust, manipulation, criminal activities, and cruelty. It is an energy of extremes, often being noted in obsessesive-compulsive behavior patterns.

THRUST LETTER: You are a private, self-contained individual. You can spend much time alone (**K**londike Pete). You dislike others prying into your personal life. You have good recuperative abilities. Your feelings are intense. You have a keen sense of awareness and are very bright. You take life seriously and are always examining your motives and actions, wanting to purge and purify yourself every chance you get. You are magnetic, can be manipulative as well as forceful and controlling. However, as a rule you are more concerned with controlling your own self than running the lives of others. You may be a late bloomer. Your close relationships tend to be with individuals who are strong, sensual, deep thinkers. You are very good at handling (and spending) their money for them.

KEY LETTER: You tend to wrap things up with insight,

shrewdness, and brute force (Kung Fu). (See thrust letter description.)

FIRST LETTER OF SURNAME: You have an aptitude for financial dealings and can handle other people's money; you will probably make more money for them than for yourself! You can get involved in a mental health career. You are insightful and thoughtful, which makes you potentially a good analyst or counselor. You see right through people—they can't fool you. Other talents indicate you would make a super sleuth, researcher, and/or mortician, being intense and able to work alone. You take everything seriously; your career *has* to hold a meaning—nothing mundane or superficial for you. You will find you can have more than one career, just like Clark Kent, a.k.a. Superman. (See thrust letter description.)

HINGE LETTER: You have a compulsion for change and rebirth in all areas of your life. You have a need to guard your health.

RANDOM LETTER: You are a no-nonsense person. You feel that if you are going to do something, you are going to do it right, all the way, or not at all. You have a penetrating mind; it is difficult to put something over on you. You require privacy and you respect the privacy of others. As a matter of fact, you can be downright secretive. You have strong intuitive abilities and a periodic need to renew yourself and change things in your life. You like to throw things away, which may include old lovers. You can be a pretty sexy character.

DOUBLE LETTER(KK): You have excellent recuperative

abilities, but you are the compulsive type. You tend to overindulge in sexual/sensual pleasures. You put much energy into making money, spending money, and enjoying luxuries. You have the ability to close doors behind you and begin anew, without ever looking back. You can be extremely stubborn, tenacious, and strong-willed. You can harness psychological power, which you may use for good or ill. Then there is the obstinate, bullheaded, paranoid side to your nature, which only comes out after dark. You should guard against being manipulative, vengeful, and jealous.

MULTIPLE LETTERS: You enjoy good physical health and an astute, insightful mind. You need to feel that whatever you do is important. For you, it is all or nothing at all.

L

SYNONYMS: Lover, Lovely, Legal, Luscious, Lazy, Languid, Liaison.

DEFINITION: This is a social energy that needs to relate, primarily on a one-to-one basis. It has a strong sense for equality, fairness, harmony, along with a flair for color, form, and beauty. It requires mental stimulation and an outlet for ideas. It can be experienced positively as romantic ideas, feelings, and involvements. It is refined, can be flirtatious, charming, and graceful. It can be experienced negatively as moodiness, laziness, vacillation, indecisiveness, dogmatism, bossiness, and egotism—L people can also tend to be judgmental and demanding.

THRUST LETTER: You have a refined, attractive appearance. You have a flair for fashion (Liberace) and a keenly developed sense of aesthetics. You are fair-minded but sometimes opinionated. You have a tendency to internalize. Your sense of self-worth is often based on how others view you. There must always be romance in your life. You are lost without a liaison. You are a social butterfly. Although essentially peace-loving, you do enjoy a good argument from time to time. Your close relationships tend to be with individuals who are outgoing, outspoken, and active.

KEY LETTER: You tend to wrap things up by being as fair as possible. You talk out all matters in order to arrive at amiable conclusions. (See thrust letter description.)

FIRST LETTER OF SURNAME: You have an aptitude for fashion design and public relations. Your diplomatic nature allows you to move in many diverse circles, which is a definite career plus. You have a knack for the law and a strong sense of justice (Sir Lancelot). You have speaking abilities as well as counseling know-how. You are happy when working with people and will do well in partnerships. (See thrust letter description.)

HINGE LETTER: You have a need to develop a sense of self-worth. You must learn to love yourself before you can love others.

RANDOM LETTER: You are social and need to have contact with people. You wish to maintain peace and harmony in your environment. You have a diplomatic flair—relationships are a must for you. You believe that you know what's best for everyone and you don't mind telling them so, yet you can be refined, charming, and gracious. You can also be lazy, indecisive, moody, stubborn, and dogmatic.

DOUBLE LETTER(LL): You hate to hurt people's feelings and find it difficult to say no. Though you may dislike being alone, you need time for yourself to regenerate, because you expend so much energy on others. Half the time you want a partner, and the other half you want to make it on your own. You want recognition for your individuality and assume that what your partner does (if you take one) is a reflection of you. You have a temper that you must work at keeping under control. You are diplomatic, fair-minded, and desire quiet, peace, and harmony in your environment. You think things over carefully before making decisions; so carefully that sometimes you never come to any decision at all.

MULTIPLE LETTERS: You are diplomatic, fair-minded, and make decisions slowly. You prefer to reevalute before coming to final conclusions.

M

SYNONYMS: Mommy, Mushy, Manipulative, Mother, Maternal, Memory, Memorabilia.

DEFINITION: This is an energy that has to feel productive, busy, needed. It is a nurturing and mothering energy, but it can easily turn from mothering to smothering—the Jewish Mother syndrome. Family ties are important. It can be experienced positively as caring, loving, and productivity. It is an energy that hates to waste time; take Mary Poppins, for example. When experienced negatively, M people can be moody, stingy, and possessive. They have trouble letting go. There is the danger of dependency, either having others too dependent on you, or your becoming overdependent on them. Cutting the umbilical cord is often difficult.

THRUST LETTER: You are a very active, busy individual. Your mind, mouth, and hands can all work at the same time. (You remind us of one of those windup toys.) You have a need to feel productive and useful. You enjoy helping others solve their problems. Your feelings and sensitivity run silent and deep—like the submarine. You have a tendency to be hyper, to overreact and worry excessively. Family ties and involvements become a major part of your life. You are money conscious. Your close relationships seem to be with individuals who are older, established, and mature.

KEY LETTER: You tend to conclude things by making sure that everyone feels secure. (See thrust letter description.)

FIRST LETTER OF SURNAME: You have an aptitude for a career in a helping and nurturing profession. You seem to draw to you people who need advice and solutions to their problems; you want to help, comfort, and understand them. You can work in a profession that takes care of the needs of people, such as the food, clothing, and housing industries. You will be happy dealing with the public or in a public service capacity. A great example of **M** surname energy is Golda Meir. (See thrust letter description.)

HINGE LETTER: You have to learn to deal with dependencies. You can cause others to be dependent on you or find yourself being dependent on others.

RANDOM LETTER: You have close ties to your family and friends. You want to take care of those in need and those with problems. You have a tendency to worry and overreact to situations, most of which have nothing to do with you. You are a home-loving, caring, nurturing individual, who has a need to keep busy and productive. You often bite off more than you can chew. You are willing to work hard to earn money and can squirrel it away quite well.

DOUBLE LETTER(MM): You must be careful to mother, and not smother. **Mommy**! You tend to be overactive, always doing something or going somewhere, never giving yourself a break. You can be overprotective, controlling, and a strict authoritarian. You have a great desire to succeed in the world, to attain status and money. You know the value of a dollar. You can be moody, clinging, inhibited, and may repress your feelings. You tend to give business a high priority. You require money for emotional security and status. You are at your best when in charge.

MULTIPLE LETTERS: You have a tendency toward hyperactivity. You can do too much for others, often overcommitting your time and energy.

N

SYNONYMS: Neat, Nitpicking, Nervous, Nagging, Nice, Nutrition, Neurosis.

DEFINITION: This is an energy that flows through well-managed, practical, everyday matters. It represents the nitty-gritty of life. It flows best through service-oriented activities, intellectual finesse, sound health practices, and hard work. It tends to be a very serious energy that deals in practicalities. ("Just give me the facts, ma'am.") It can be experienced positively as discriminating qualities, exactness, conscientiousness, an analytical approach to life, the handling of details. Negatively it can be experienced as inhibitions, isolationism, destructive self-criticism, as well as nervous chatter, obsessive worry over matters that are beyond control, and heavy guilt trips.

THRUST LETTER: You are self-critical. You do not always express your own desires, sometimes putting the needs of others above your own. You get satisfaction out of working and doing a job well. You seek perfection in yourself and others, but may not admit to this. You can be orderly, neat, exacting, self-discliplined, or a nit-picker who can waste time with nonproductive routines and details. You have an interest in health matters. You want to feel needed. You worry too much. Your close relationships tend to be with individuals who let you do things for them.

KEY LETTER: You wish to conclude matters in a conscientious, efficient manner. You have a need to be in control. That nice, neat, hypochondriacal nut of *The Odd Couple* fame reminds us of you. (See thrust letter description.)

FIRST LETTER OF SURNAME: You have an aptitude for health and service work, along the lines of Florence Nightingale. You can be exacting, meticulous, organized, and mentally compartmentalized. Very little gets past your analytical, inquiring mind. You may find yourself in careers such as accounting or financial analysis or any field in which attention to detail is required. Your interests in pets and your strong service orientation give you much in common with Noah. (See thrust letter description.)

HINGE LETTER: You may have a compulsion to serve, but you must learn to give service wisely. You can suffer in silence, playing the martyr. You must guard against falling into the trap of hypochondria.

RANDOM LETTER: You are a hard worker once you get going. You think things through very carefully before deciding what to do or how to do it. You plan your strategy well. You have the ability to handle details. You can be quite health conscious, orderly, organized, exacting, and fussy. You can burden yourself with guilt. You take pride in a job well done. You want to help others and to be of service. You are quite discerning, discriminating, and shy, even though you enjoy talking and socializing.

DOUBLE LETTER(NN): You may be super-critical of yourself and others. You can go on health kicks or totally neglect your health. You are capable of holding down two jobs, one of which may be in a health profession. You go to extremes, either being very industrious or very lazy—

though most of the time, it's industrious. It bothers you to leave something undone, so you will forgo leisure time to complete a task. You may find yourself leaning toward escapism, avoiding facing issues, and spending more time in your head than in reality. You may find yourself drawn to people who need your help. You do many tasks at once, not necessarily in any sequential order.

MULTIPLE LETTERS: You are efficient, can be a workaholic, are very organized and overcritical.

O

SYNONYMS: **O**bstinate, **O**rganized, **O**stentatious, **O**bsolete, **O**bsessive.

DEFINITION: This is an energy of the subconscious mind, centering around your desires and your security needs. You can experience it positively as protectiveness, loyalty, and inner strength. There is an interest in occult, metaphysical, and spiritual matters. This energy is nurturant and has close family bonds. It can be experienced negatively in obsessive, controlling, and manipulative tendencies. There can be a need to control the lives of those around you.

THRUST LETTER: You are tenacious and you never give up. You can cling to the home and family for the security they provide. You are intense and take life seriously. You have powerful emotions and tend to channel them into your work. You can be magnetic and a source of healing power. Your close relationships tend mostly to be with individuals who are determined and sensual and who willingly work hard for money. You are attracted to the powerful and strong, like **O**live **O**il, for example.

KEY LETTER: You tend to wrap things up in an efficient, no-nonsense manner. You put things behind you, once and for all, when you're finished with them. (See thrust letter description.)

FIRST LETTER OF SURNAME: You have an aptitude for the study and practice of psychology. You can work well with children or in an area that deals with their concerns. You also have financial acumen . . . just like Aristotle **O**nassis. Your career is important to you; it must hold meaning and significance. You will not work in an area you believe to be frivolous. You can have more than one career in your lifetime, but you'll always seek a challenge. You are an excellent problem solver and a great troubleshooter. (See thrust letter description.)

HINGE LETTER: You have a need to regenerate; making changes in your life is an ongoing process. Lighten up! You tend to be too serious and sometimes too manipulative.

RANDOM LETTER: You have strong emotions, which you try to direct into constructive uses. You have a highly developed sixth sense. When it comes to your loved ones, you are very loyal and protective. You have strong dependency needs, which you try to control. You have a tendency toward compulsive behavior. You are intense and put all of your energy into everything you do. You can be stubborn, fixed in your opinions, and slow to make changes. However, you are a powerhouse when set in motion.

DOUBLE LETTER(OO): You can be self-indulgent and have a strong drive to make money and gain power (J. Edgar H**oo**ver). You can be either very lazy and placid, or exhibit incredible energy that drives you—and others—crazy, but may well bring great achievements. You may find that you are attracted to people who wish to direct your life and who can be jealous of your friends and your need for solitude. You are sexy, sensual, and possessive.

MULTIPLE LETTERS: You can handle finances and business matters, and enjoy solving problems. You are inclined to look for hidden messages, meanings, and motives. This implies that you are either very cautious and suspicious by nature, or paranoid. Which is it?

P

SYNONYMS: **P**assive, **P**ensive, **P**olitical, **P**articular, **P**artnership.

DEFINITION: This is an energy of thought in action. Beauty, balance, and harmony are all required in your environment. This energy must have social contacts . . . and romance. It can be experienced positively as amiability, diplomacy, independence, and individuality. The use of logic is strong. Fighting for a just cause is a common **P** experience, and working with people on a one-to-one level is a **P** talent. Negatively it can be experienced as procrastination, laziness, stubbornness, self-centeredness, and indecisiveness. At times it can be very judgmental, bossy, and demanding.

THRUST LETTER: You are social and peace-loving, always wanting to get along yet somehow managing to make waves. You do not work well in unharmonious conditions. You have a temper, a low threshold for frustration, and can be opinionated. Relationships are paramount for you; however, you must maintain your independence and individuality. You are a nonconformist who conforms, having interests in unusual areas. You march to your own drummer. In many instances, especially if you are female, you tend to be a very physical person with a strong sense of self. People are aware of your presence. If you are male, there appears to be a soft quality to your nature. Your close relationships tend to be with physical, sometimes forceful, pioneering, determined, and idealistic people.

KEY LETTER: You tend to wrap things up by being fair, logical, reasonable, and equitable. (See thrust letter description.)

FIRST LETTER OF SURNAME: You have an aptitude for the law, public speaking, and counseling. Your diplomatic skills can be put to career use. Your creativity runs along the lines of design, fashion, and interior decorating. Anything innovative is up your alley. You are an idea person. (See thrust letter description.)

HINGE LETTER: You have a need to learn to face conflict, not avoid it for the sake of peace. You must remember that there are kinds of harmony that can only be gained through conflict.

RANDOM LETTER: You are partner-oriented, sociable, and you desire harmonious conditions in your surroundings. You're protective of your own individuality and want to avoid losing yourself to an overpowering partner for the sake of a relationship. You are peace-loving, seeking harmony and balance in all you do. You tend to be patient unless pushed too far; then you can exhibit your temper. Justice and fair play are important to you; diplomacy, tact, and sound logic are your forte.

DOUBLE LETTER(PP): You want peace at any price, even to the point of fighting for it. You can be quite moody, changeable, as well as foolhardy, and/or daring, taking actions without forethought. You can rush ahead, not taking the needs of others into consideration, or you can bend over backward to keep the peace, never doing what you yourself want.

MULTIPLE LETTERS: You can be a sophist, an arbitrator, a diplomat, as well as a social butterfly and the hostess with the mostess (Emily Post, Madame Pompadour).

Q

SYNONYMS: Quick, Quizzical, Quipster, Quaint, Quest, Quiver.

DEFINITION: This is an energy of expansion. You can be carried away by enthusiasm, by the need to explore new ground, to gain knowledge, and to find out what the future has in store. This energy is adventurous, idealistic, philosophical, and moral, all at the same time. It can be experienced positively as a fun-loving nature, an adventurous spirit, and an open mind. Negatively it can be experienced as scattered or unrealistic thinking, bigotry, narrow-mindedness, and scarcasm.

THRUST LETTER: You are never at a loss for what to do and what to say. It is difficult for others to keep up with you. You are excitable, optimistic, romantic, and idealistic, like a modern-day Don Quixote. You like to take on challenges and causes, like Quincy, M.E. Your close relationships tend to be with people who are diversified, interesting, and talkative.

KEY LETTER: You tend to wrap things up by hoping for the best.

FIRST LETTER OF SURNAME: You have a quick, imaginative mind and a gift for gab. It is hard to outtalk or outthink you. You might find a job in publicity, publishing, or sales. You are sports-minded and can work in that lucrative area. You are a promoter by nature, always thinking big . . . sometimes too big. You thrive on excitement, challenge, and quest. You enjoy travel and a job that keeps you on the move, whether by land, sea, or air. (See thrust letter description.)

HINGE LETTER: You have a need to learn moderation. You are a cockeyed optimist.

RANDOM LETTER: You are alert, sassy, quick, and enthusiastic, tending toward excessive excitability and optimism. You are expansive, adventurous, can be foolhardy, impetuous, and very easily bored. Your idealism and principled beliefs can carry you away from the realities of life. You are always ready to think the best and the biggest. You are a fun-loving, open, idea person.

DOUBLE LETTER(QQ): You can be moralistic, scattered in your thinking, and get a swelled head. You are a busy person, and it is difficult for others to keep pace. They give up and leave you to do your own things—which is what you really want anyway.

MULTIPLE LETTERS: You are quite active, excitable, enthusiastic, and often busy and mixed up.

R

SYNONYMS: **R**eason, **R**ational, **R**esourceful, **R**estless.

DEFINITION: Thought-directed action is what this energy is all about. It is rational, logical, and thrives on challenge and forward movement. It needs to improve things and can be experienced positively as enthusiasm, idealism, and ambition. *It is assertion through the use of reason.* The intellect is quick and sharp. Thoughts are put into action with very little hesitancy. Negatively it can demonstrate itself as foolhardiness, impatience, quick temper, impulsiveness, and indecisiveness as well as a tendency to avoid or rationalize emotions.

THRUST LETTER: You are self-reliant, outgoing, pioneering, innovative, and forward-thinking. You are willing to take actions and risks once you are set on a course. You have an active, logical, bright mind. You are determined and will fight for what you want. At times you have no patience and a low tolerance for nonsense and nonproductive activity. You weigh and balance all of your decisions. The strength of your mental abilities surfaces around age twenty-eight. You can make impersonal decisions but have difficulty on a personal level. You handle thoughts much better than emotions. In many cases, **R** men are refined, fashion-conscious, charming, disarming, and at their best when involved in a relationship. **R** women are quite independent, capable, responsible, and may exhibit masculine qualities on the exterior and hide their more feminine traits. Most of your close relationships tend to be with individuals who are social, intelligent, and attractive.

KEY LETTER: You tend to wrap things up by taking actions only after careful consideration. (See thrust letter description.)

FIRST LETTER OF SURNAME: You have an aptitude for solving problems, communicating, and leading. You can be in the forefront of any field you enter. You thrive on a challenge and enjoy breaking new ground. You are ambitious, career-oriented, and do not let setbacks stand in your way. You are an idea person, never at a loss for plans and projects. You can take direction from others, but work best on your own. Ideally you should be your own boss. You tend to be a super-achiever, enjoying starting things and moving on to the next challenge. After you have learned all there is for you to learn in one field, you become bored and seek something new. Your eyes and ears are always watching and listening for what comes next. (See thrust letter description.)

HINGE LETTER: You must use your intellect to its fullest and overcome any feelings of insecurity regarding your mind. You have a fear of taking risks. This fear will be overcome in time.

RANDOM LETTER: You have the ability to take thought-directed actions. You are a positive, forward-thinking individual who can handle a challenge. You are logical, action-oriented, and thrive on advancement. You have a need to improve upon circumstances. You are assertive, especially through the use of reason, as well as enthusiastic, idealistic, impatient, and impulsive. You can have a quick temper.

DOUBLE LETTERS(RR): You have a quick temper and need a release for your super-charged mental energies. Your mind is constantly working, even when sleeping. You can have difficulty dealing with slower-thinking individuals. You seek out relationships but have problems cooperating as you are ten steps ahead in your thinking. You lack patience, wanting everything to happen immediately. You can be pushy and bossy, or may find yourself attracted to forceful individuals. You never put all of your eggs in one basket, always providing an alternative. You are willing to take chances; but don't let yourself get carried away like Harry Houdini.

MULTIPLE LETTERS: You have an extremely active mind. You are never at a loss for things to do or say. You are a leader, a take-charge person.

S

SYNONYMS: Success, Status, Social Standing, Security, Sex, Sensuality, Solidity.

DEFINITION: This is an energy that seeks success and a place in society. It is status conscious and knows how to make money. It can be experienced positively as achievement, business acumen, and just for for status, authority, and money. This energy needs responsibility, respect, social trappings, and recognition. It can be experienced negatively as miserliness, bossiness, harshness, depression, moodiness, coldness, shyness, and antisocial behavior.

THRUST LETTER: Your status, as well as your ability to earn money and be self-supporting, is very important to you. You want to be a big fish in a big pond. Being practical, though, you will settle for a little pond, if it is the only one in the neighborhood. You tend to be a super-achiever: not an overachiever, but a super-star. You take life and yourself very seriously. Can you identify with Superman? You want *big bucks*. You are highly sexual, but you do not project this outwardly. You and Sigmund Freud have much in common. Most of your close involvements tend to be with individuals who are emotional, nurturant, and who let you take care of them . . . which you don't mind, as this satisfies your need to be important.

KEY LETTER: You tend to wrap things up in a practical, no-nonsense manner, and in such a way as to make you look good. (See thrust letter description.)

FIRST LETTER OF SURNAME: You have an aptitude

for business and financial matters. You are capable of cool, detached, unemotional handling of responsibility, à la Mr. Spock of the SS *Enterprise*. Your career and status are very important to you, and in them achievement is a must in order for you to maintain your self-respect. You do care what the neighbors think. Your concern with finances makes you a good money manager. You need a secure monetary basis from which to operate. You will work long and hard to achieve your goals. You will be happiest when in charge and/or running your own business. (See thrust letter description.)

HINGE LETTER: You must learn the true value of material gains and status. You have a need to earn money to prove your success to society and to yourself as well.

RANDOM LETTER: Status, achievement, reputation, and money are all important to you. You measure your successes in terms of your earning capabilities. You have a strong sensuous quality to your nature. You have good organizational abilities, and seek quality as opposed to quantity. You push yourself to the limits and then some. You can go too far, as did Samson when he met Delilah.

DOUBLE LETTER(SS): You can have two careers at the same time. You have deep financial security needs, which can be experienced as a fear of poverty or loss of possessions. There is a tendency to overwork or isolate yourself in order to avoid close personal ties. To some people you can be miserly, bossy, cold, controlling, yet to others, loving, caring, and giving. You are fiercely independent in order to overcome deep-rooted dependencies.

MULTIPLE LETTERS: You are very conscious of your body image, your money image, and your sex appeal.

T

SYNONYMS: **T**ruth, Doubting **T**homas, **T**ireless, **T**ouchy, **T**alkative, **T**esty, **T**acky.

DEFINITION: This is an energy of feelings, inner knowledge, intuitions, and imagination. It is essentially mental and seeks knowledge of abstract truths and principles. It can operate within a cosmic framework. **T** energy may be experienced positively as enjoyment of sensual pleasure and beauty, emotionalism, idealism, sensitivity, and compassion. It is poetic, obscure, spiritual, peaceful, and kind. This energy can be very private, self-contained, and skeptical. It may be experienced negatively as confusion, deceit, delusion, and escapism. Its extreme range of negative expressions include neediness, depression, and self-pity.

THRUST LETTER: You are overly sensitive and you love your privacy. You try to conceal your feelings, but this is not so readily done. You never forget an injustice. It is easy for you to fall into a savior/martyr role. You often try too hard to please others. Your deep emotions flow through your creative endeavors, and your rich inner life is more real to you than your outer life. Spiritual striving and a search for knowledge keep you going. You have psychic abilities. Your close relationships tend to be with individuals who are exacting, practical, and who have difficulty drawing close emotionally, people who at times can become real pains. You are likely to be attracted to foreigners. (You know: You Tarzan, me Jane.)

KEY LETTER: You tend to wrap things up by using your intuition and doing what feels right, even if that means making a quick exit. (See thrust letter description.)

FIRST LETTER OF SURNAME: You have an aptitude for health care or for helping those who cannot help themselves. You are creative; your artistic talents can be put to use in any field. Think, for example, of Tchaikovsky, Toulouse-Lautrec, Twinkletoes, Mark Twain, and Elizabeth Taylor. Your visions and fantasies will come in handy for work in design, the media, and publicity. Travel intrigues you, which may lead you to international affairs . . . both business and personal. Your strong urge for freedom is paramount in your job selections. You need mental and emotional space, even if you cannot have actual physical space. (See thrust letter description.)

HINGE LETTER: You have a need to learn to substitute faith in place of fear. You need to find a balance between your feelings and your thoughts.

RANDOM LETTER: You are idealistic, intuitive, sensitive, skeptical, and creative. You desire privacy. You seek knowledge of abstract truths, belief systems and principles, all of which operate within a universal framework. Your deep, compassionate feelings demonstrate themselves poetically. Your sensitive nature often gets the best of you, sometimes causing moodiness and depression. You seek answers. You have been known to be a Doubting Thomas.

DOUBLE LETTER(TT): You are highly intuitive and overly sensitive. You may have problems differentiating between imagination and logic. Do you sometimes feel you live in the Twilight Zone, or inside your TV set? You are skeptical, yet compassionate, sometimes to a fault. You are humane and can't stand suffering. You are service-oriented, in fact a compulsive do-gooder. You can be efficient, organized, and often highly critical of yourself and others. You love small animals.

MULTIPLE LETTERS: You have an investigative mind. You keep your personal life private.

U

SYNONYMS: Understanding, Universality, Unity, Utopia, Undermining.

DEFINITION: This is an energy of idealism, kindness, generosity, and expansion. This energy acts in big ways. It is optimistic, to say the least. It holds a strong sense of spirituality. Experienced positively, it is outgoing, sincere, versatile, excitable, expansive, and lucky. Negatively it may be experienced as grandiosity or bigotry; U people may be opinionated loudmouths, tactless, and selfish.

THRUST LETTER: Your mind runs to humanitarianism and your thoughts are mainly in the future. You have a charitable nature, giving much time to worthy causes. You are often generous to a fault. Much of your energy is expended in the search for a viable philosophy upon which to base your life. You spend more time outside your home than in it. You dream of romance and adventure, faraway places. Your close involvements tend to be with individuals who are diversified, good conversationalists, and who enjoy travel.

KEY LETTER: You're a pace-setter. You always try to be of service.

FIRST LETTER OF SURNAME: You have an aptitude for teaching, the law, and religion. You want to put your efforts into something that counts. If you teach, you wish to share your knowledge and at the same time continue learning yourself. If you choose a career in the law, you will champion the underdog, fight for just causes, trying to bring equity to all. Your religious endeavors can lead you to deep study and spiritual searching. Your intuitive understanding allows you to deal well with all kinds of individuals. You may find yourself placed in situations where you work with foreigners, governments, and trade. You will be happy in a career that lets you travel. (See thrust letter description.)

HINGE LETTER: You need to learn the true meaning of giving. You must work at keeping your mind open, as you can be prejudiced.

RANDOM LETTER: You exhibit qualities of philosophical understanding, sympathy, and generosity. You have a humanitarian streak. Your intuitive understanding allows you to deal well with all kinds of individuals. You wish to improve the human condition in some way. By nature, you think big, are optimistic and expansive. However, you may be inclined toward sarcasm, because you're often opinionated and tactless. But, of course, you only say things to people for their own good.

DOUBLE LETTER (UU): You can be either generous to a fault or very stingy. You may have to learn how to give from the heart and not the pocket. You tend to go too far with explanations, and can be inconsistent, flippant, and scattered. You have the gift of gab and a certain tendency to stretch the truth. You have natural acting abilities and are able to learn quickly, especially by imitation. You reject limitations and boundaries. You positively ignore all negatives as well as the facts, if they do not fit into your schemes. You take life by the tail.

MULTIPLE LETTERS: You can be very up or very down, very generous or quite self-indulgent.

V

SYNONYMS: Variety, Versatility, Vivacious, Vexing.

DEFINITION: This is a detached mental energy that is objective, cohesive, and persevering. It requires mental growth and stimulation. This energy is group-oriented and community-minded. It can be experienced positively as individuality and independence, and works best on its own. It is unconventional, advanced, has leadership abilities, and can acquire technical skills. *This energy exhibits strong* *loner instincts;* yet **V** people seem to need others as their source of excitement and amusement, and can, on the negative side, be stubborn, eccentric, and shocking—simply for the sake of being shocking. They can exhibit erratic and highly unpredictable behavior patterns. Their energies are antitraditional, nonconformist, and antisocial.

THRUST LETTER: You need independence, and desire to handle your problems alone. You have difficulty getting close emotionally, instead maintaining distance and autonomy in relationships—even though you may not care to admit this. You march to your own drummer. You do not want to be told what to do and dislike telling others what they should do. You work best on your own and thrive on a challenge. Your close involvements tend to be with individuals who are outgoing, friendly, gregarious, dramatic, and who mind their own business. Only you are allowed to be nosy.

KEY LETTER: You wrap things up by solving the problem, having your own way, and walking away. You won't be fenced in. (See thrust letter description.)

FIRST LETTER OF SURNAME: You have an aptitude for science and technology. If you choose, you can involve yourself in engineering or medicine . . . any of the advanced sciences. You are eclectic, versatile, and enjoy learning new techniques. You need freedom of body and mind, especially because you get bored quite easily. Therefore, you may find it difficult to stay with one job. You can't feel confined. You dislike taking orders.

Your inclination is to be dramatic à la Rudolph Valentino. (See thrust letter description.)

HINGE LETTER: You must learn how to follow in order to learn how to lead.

RANDOM LETTER: You are excitable, full of ideas and diverse interests. You have many friends. By nature, you are unconventional. You possess leadership abilities and can master technical skills. Your need to be free is strong, yet you often take on responsibilities that bring restrictions. You are versatile and seek stimulation, amusement, and the unique in all you do.

DOUBLE LETTER(VV): You want to be boss and usually are. No one can tell you what to do. You can see beyond the immediate situation and evaluate matters on a broad range. Your makeup requires that you shine and receive love as well as attention on a steady basis. You are idealistic and creative. When you need to make changes, you make waves instead; change does not come easy for you.

MULTIPLE LETTERS: Your disposition is that of a social reformer/climber. You may find it difficult to handle intimacy. Let's face it. You love humanity; it's people you can't stand.

W

SYNONYMS: Willful, Wonderful, Wonderment, Wild, Wishful.

DEFINITION: This is an energy of pride and ego. The

sense of self must be experienced and acknowledged by the world. This is an energy that must be expressed through love and creativity. Ego strengths and weaknesses are active. It is a dramatic energy that enjoys challenge and wants to be on top. It can be experienced positively as a cheery, sunny disposition, with a very giving, loving nature. It can be experienced negatively as false pride, egotism, snobbishness, willfulness, and domination.

THRUST LETTER: You are determined to prove yourself. You're sensitive, and, if rejected, you tend to internalize your hurt and isolate yourself. Then it becomes difficult for you to come out of your shell. When you do your thing, you wish to receive recognition for your efforts. You are fun loving, gregarious, and the life of any party. You can be romantic and will do anything to make the object of your affections happy. You have a need to express your creativity. Walt Disney certainly did his W energy proud. You relate well to children. Your close relationships tend to be with individuals who are detached, unconventional, and who may shy away from intimacy.

KEY LETTER: You tend to wrap things up by being willful, determined, dramatic, and sometimes with a me-first attitude. (See thrust letter description.)

FIRST LETTER OF SURNAME: You have an aptitude for leading, public speaking, and creative endeavors. Your career achievements are tied to your ego needs; you do not separate the two. You should do well in public service, politics (George Washington, Wendell Wilkie, and Woodrow Wilson), the entertainment business (Mae West), a glamour industry, or in sports. Your leadership abilities are strong and you enjoy being the center of attention. You enjoy making others happy; therefore, working in places of amusement and leisure activities will bring satisfaction. (See thrust letter description.)

HINGE LETTER: You have a need to learn humility. You can fall victim to false pride.

RANDOM LETTER: You want to shine and somehow stand out in the crowd. You are proud, willful, and determined to succeed. You are creative and should not let this gift go to waste. You are dramatic and enjoy challenges, especially the kind that will make others notice you. You have a positive, cheery disposition and are kind, sharing, and idealistic. You love a good time. However, you can be bossy, snobbish, tacky, and the party clown—the one with the lampshade on his head.

DOUBLE LETTER(WW): You can be rebellious, attention-starved, erratic, eccentric, and you love to play the role of the crazy genius. You may find yourself being overly concerned with what others think, or at the opposite extreme, you may exhibit antisocial behavior. You require recognition, appreciation, and strokes. Nice baby . . .

MULTIPLE LETTERS: You have unfailing determination. You are always ready for a good time—"hail fellow well met."

X

SYNONYMS: Extreme, Extravagant, Exaggeration, Exhaustive, Extensive, Excitement, **X** marks the spot.

DEFINITION: This energy flexes the mental muscles. The mind is exercised and expended through the use of imagination and intuition. **X** never lets the mind relax. It is a boundless, mystifying, multidimensional energy, which can be experienced positively as diverse talents, abilities, and interests. Your creative imagination and sense of curiosity are highly developed. **X** energy can be experienced negatively as confusion, ambivalence, and lack of direction and can fall prey to scattered efforts that never lead to solid conclusions.

THRUST LETTER: You are almost too talented, lacking the organizational skills to handle your genius. You need a manager, not a trainer. You are too smart, and you know this is true because you tend to confuse yourself. You can be hyper, and only a person like Xavier Cugat can keep pace with you. Your close relationships are with individuals who are, needless to say, active, expressive, expansive, and crazy.

KEY LETTER: You cover all possible avenues and routes. You can overdo, overtalk, and overreact. (See thrust letter description.)

FIRST LETTER OF SURNAME: You have an aptitude for salesmanship, acting, and verbal abuse. You are mentally active, possessing a quick wit and an intuitive mind. You think of schemes and ideas. The trick for you is to slow down long enough to put your ideas into action. You can be a go-between, an agent, anyone who brings people together. You will be happy in a career that provides excitement and diversity. (See thrust letter description.)

HINGE LETTER: You must learn concentration and patience. You scatter your energies. Take up meditation.

RANDOM LETTER: You're basically a diversified, multifaceted, multidimensional, talented person. (Seems almost too good to be true.) However, you can have so many talents that nothing gets put to use. You tend to jump from one thing to another. If you find yourself with no direction, take things slowly, one step at a time. Otherwise you'll make yourself anxious, uptight, crazy, when, in fact, you should be highly creative, innovative, and clever.

DOUBLE LETTER(XX): You lean toward being hyperactive and super-sensitive. You're an introvert who enjoys isolation. You worry, and when you are not worrying, you are flying high. You are full of visions, ideas, and ideals. Sometimes you lose the differentiation between your visions and what is actually happening out there in the real world.

MULTIPLE LETTERS: You are subject to excessive mental stimulation and confusion.

Y

SYNONYMS: Yin/Yang, Yen/money, Youth-giving.

DEFINITION: This is an energy of independence and

success. It thrives on attainment, status, and monetary achievements. It can be experienced positively as prudence, discipline, masterfulness, practicality, perseverence, and responsibility. Negatively this energy can be seen as snobbishness, stinginess, stubbornness, insecurity, and a tendency to worry.

THRUST LETTER: You prefer to do things your own way and on your own terms. You have leadership qualities and the ability to take independent action. You are not afraid to take on responsibility. Money and status are synonymous to you—you want both. You tend to hook up with individuals who are nurturant, emotional, and clinging.

KEY LETTER: You are stubborn and want everything your way. You are fiercely independent and success-oriented, very like Henry Ford. (See thrust letter description.)

FIRST LETTER OF SURNAME: You have an aptitude for executive work, have administrative abilities, and should be in charge. You hate to take orders and love to give them. (You can give it but can't take it.) Your career goals, reputation, and bank account are very important to you. You must feel monetarily secure. You will do well in your own business as you really must be an independent agent. (See thrust letter description.)

HINGE LETTER: You must learn to give the same freedom to others that you want for yourself. You may have difficulty handling authority or authority figures.

RANDOM LETTER: You seek out positions of authority, responsibility, status, and ways of achieving monetary success *all in an attempt to overcome deep feelings of* *insecurity*. You must believe that you are in charge of your life. You are willing to work long and hard to achieve your goals. You can be disciplined, self-controlled, calculating, and frugal; or to put it another way, you can be conniving and stingy. You tend to put business before pleasure. You dislike taking orders. Independence is your personal byword. (See thrust letter description.)

DOUBLE LETTERS(YY): Have you noticed that you are surrounded by individuals who depend on you for both emotional and financial support? On reflection, you may discover that you are dependent on their dependencies. They make you feel like a big shot. All kidding aside, you are a warm person who wishes to help people and take care of them, which may curtail some of your freedoms. This can cause conflict.

MULTIPLE LETTERS: You may be too serious, stiff, and unbending. Therefore, you can be a stick-in-the-mud and a sourpuss.

Z

SYNONYMS: Zen, Zodiac, Zigzag, Zany, Zombie.

DEFINITION: This is an energy of fate. It is a reaping of past deeds, whether in this lifetime or from a time prior to birth—if you believe in that sort of thing. **Z** is a letter of karma in action. As you sow, so shall you reap . . . cause and effect. It is an energy of hidden fortune, hidden strengths, hidden misfortune, and hidden weaknesses. It can be experienced positively as financial luck, a knack for being in the right place at the right time. You have spirit guides. Negatively it can be experienced as the fickle hand of fate. It can bring misfortune or bad luck. The person carrying the letter **Z** can cause his or her own bad luck through hidden motives that may cause self-undoing. This is truly an energy of the spirit. **Z** must be respected. Do not add it to a name lightly.

THRUST LETTER: Your luck is either very good or very bad. There can be unlucky breaks through no fault of your own, or misfortune due to fear, lack of faith, or karmic lessons. You can be your own worst enemy. You are compassionate, psychic, creative, sensitive, impressionable, and sly. You can fall into a savior/martyr role through choice or chance. Your close relationships tend to be with individuals who need your help and seem always to have health problems, money troubles, or general malaise.

KEY LETTER: You go with the flow, often just floating along with the stream, or on the wind, or in the clouds, or out in space. . . . (See thrust letter description.)

FIRST LETTER OF SURNAME: You have an aptitude for artistic, creative pursuits and the theater. Take a bow, Mr. Florenz Ziegfeld. You will do well in public service and health care work. Institutional work is another area for you. Secretly you know you would be ecstatic if you did no work at all, ever. (See thrust letter description.)

HINGE LETTER: You must learn to accept your gift of protection from the "gods." Otherwise you might cause your own undoing. You will indulge in guilt, self-pity, and neurosis. You can replace your fears with faith.

RANDOM LETTER: You have intuitive abilities; you are inwardly knowing and are protected by higher forces. You can tap these powers as a means of gaining the knowledge you seek. Fate may deal you a dirty hand, but you are able to rise to the occasion. You are a private, behind-the-scenes person who can become a channel for helping others. But beware of being a doormat; it is too easy to take advantage of you.

DOUBLE LETTER(ZZ): You strive for peace and quiet, yet often find yourself surrounded by noise and confusion. You try to get yourself out of these situations, without much success, usually because they are in your own home. You are community-minded and service-oriented. You have deep feelings, spiritual insight, and a desire to hide.

MULTIPLE LETTERS: You can be overly sensitive, secretive, and fearful.

5

How Sexy Is Your Name?

To learn just what your name reveals about your sex appeal—what turns you on, off, and over—look to the definitions below for both *the first and last letters of your given name and/or first name used*. While you're at it, why not see what the letters have to say about your mate or lover?

A: You are not particularly romantic, but you are interested in action. You mean business. With you, what you see is what you get. You have no patience for flirting and can't be bothered with someone who is trying to be coy, cute, demure, and subtly enticing. You are an up-front person. When it comes to sex, it's action that counts, not obscure hints. Your mate's physical attractiveness is important to you. You find the chase and challenge of the "hunt" invigorating. You are passionate and sexual, as well as being much more adventurous than you appear; however, you do not go around advertising these qualities. Your physical needs are your primary concern.

B: You give off vibes of lazy sensuality. You enjoy being romanced, wined, and dined. You are very happy to receive gifts as an expression of the affection of your lover. You want to be pampered and know how to pamper your mate. You are private in your expression of endearments, and particular when it comes to lovemaking. You will hold off until everything meets with your approval. You can control your appetite and abstain from sex if need be. You require new sensations and experiences. You are willing to experiment.

C: You are a very social individual and it is important to you to have a relationship. You require closeness and togetherness. You must be able to talk to your sex partner—before, during, and after. You want the object of your affection to be socially acceptable and good-looking. You see your lover as a friend and companion. You are most sexual and sensual, needing someone to appreciate and almost worship you. When this cannot be achieved, you have the ability to go for long periods without sexual activity. You are an expert at controlling your desires and doing without.

CH: You are a romantic and a fantasizer. Moonlight and candles are your thing. You don't always see your lovers as they really are, but as you wish them to be; you idealize your lovers. You're attracted to intellect, wit, and loquaciousness. You require your lover to be as much a debating partner as a sex partner. Your relationships tend to be not only dramatic, but traumatic. You are an intense individual and lover.

D: Once you get it into your head that you want someone, you move full steam ahead in pursuit. You do not give up your quest easily. You are nurturing and caring. If someone has a problem, this turns you on. You are highly sexual, passionate, loyal, and intense in your involvements, sometimes possessive and jealous. Sex to you is a pleasure to be enjoyed. You are stimulated by the eccentric and unusual, having a free and open attitude.

E: Your greatest need is to talk. If your date is not a good listener, you have trouble relating. A person must be intellectually stimulating, or you are not interested sexually. You need a friend for a lover and a companion for a bedmate. You hate disharmony and disruption, but you do enjoy a good argument once in a while—it seems to stir things up. You flirt a lot, for the challenge is more important than the sexual act for you. But once you give your heart away, you are uncompromisingly loyal. When you don't have a good lover to fall asleep with, you will fall asleep with a good book. (Sometimes you prefer a good book.)

F: You are idealistic and romantic, putting your lover on a pedestal. You look for the very best mate you can find. You are a flirt, yet once committed, you are very loyal.

You are sensuous, sexual, and privately passionate. Publicly you can be showy, extravagant, and gallant. You are a born romantic. Dramatic love scenes are a favorite fantasy pastime. You can be a most generous lover.

G: You are fastidious, seeking perfection within yourself and your lover. You respond to a lover who is your intellectual equal or superior, and one who can enhance your status. You are sensuous and know how to reach the peak of erotic stimulation, because you work at it meticulously. You can be extremely active sexually—that is, when you find the time. Your duties and responsibilities take precedence. You may have difficulty getting emotionally close to a lover, but no trouble getting close sexually.

H: You seek out a mate who can enhance your reputation and your earning ability. You will be very generous to your lover once you have attained a commitment. Your gifts are actually an investment in your partner. Before the commitment, though, you tend to be frugal in your spending and dating habits, and equally as cautious in your sexual involvements. You are a sensual and patient lover.

I: You have a great need to be loved, appreciated . . . even worshipped. You enjoy luxury, sensuality, and pleasures of the flesh. You seek out lovers who know what they are doing. You are not interested in an amateur, unless that amateur wants a tutor. You are fussy and exacting about having your desires satisfied. You are willing to experiment and try new modes of sexual expression. You are bored easily and thus require sexual adventure and change.

You are more sensual than sexual, but you are sometimes downright lustful.

J: You are blessed with a great deal of physical energy. When it is used for lovemaking, there is nothing to stop you, except maybe the stamina of your partner. (You could have danced all night.) You respond to the thrill of the chase and the challenge of the mating game. You can carry on great romances in your head. At heart you are a roamer and need to set out on your own every so often. You will carry on long-distance relationships with ease. You are idealistic and need to believe in love. The sex act seems to satisfy a need to be nurtured deep within.

K: You are secretive, self-contained, and shy. You are very sexy, sensual, and passionate, but you do not let on about this. Only in intimate privacy will this part of your nature reveal itself. When it gets down to the nitty-gritty, you are an expert. You know all the little tricks of the trade, can play any role or any game, and take your love life very seriously. You don't fool around. You have the patience to wait for the right person to come along.

L: You can be very romantic, attached to the glamour of love. Having a partner is of paramount importance to you. You are free in your expression of love and are willing to take chances, try new sexual experiences and partners, provided it's all in good taste. Brains turn you on. You must feel that your partner is intellectually stimulating, otherwise you will find it difficult to sustain the relationship. You require loving, cuddling, wining, and dining to know that you're appreciated.

M: You are emotional and intense. When involved in a relationship, you throw your entire being into it. Nothing stops you; there are no holds barred. You are all-consuming and crave someone who is equally passionate and intense. You believe in total sexual freedom. You are willing to try anything and everything. Your supply of sexual energy is inexhaustible. You enjoy mothering your mate.

N: You may appear innocent, unassuming, and shy; but we know that appearances can lie. When it comes to sex, you are no novice, but something of a skilled technician. You can easily go to extremes, though, running the gamut from insatiability to boredom with the whole idea of sex. You can be highly critical of your mate, seeking perfection in both of you. It is not easy to find someone who can meet your standards. You have difficulty expressing emotions and drawing close to lovers.

O: You are very interested in sexual activities, yet secretive about your desires and shy. You can rechannel much of your sexual energies into making money and/or seeking power. You can easily have extended periods of celibacy. You are a passionate, compassionate, sexual lover, requiring the same qualities from your mate. Sex is serious business; thus you demand intensity, diversity, and are willing to try anything or anyone. Sometimes your passions turn to possessiveness, which must be kept in check.

P: You are very conscious of social proprieties. You wouldn't think of doing anything that might harm your image or reputation. Appearances count. Therefore, you require a good-looking partner. You also require an intelligent partner. Oddly enough, you may view your partner as your enemy . . . a good fight stimulates those sex vibes. You are relatively free of sexual hangups. You are willing to experiment and try new ways of doing things. You are very social and sensual; you enjoy flirting and need a good deal of physical gratification.

Q: You require constant activity and stimulation. You have tremendous reserves of physical energy. It is not easy for a partner to keep up with you sexually or otherwise. You are an enthusiastic lover, being attracted to ethnic people. You need romance, hearts and flowers, and lots of conversation to turn you on and keep you going.

R: You are a no-nonsense, action-oriented individual. You need someone who can keep pace with you and who is your intellectual equal—the smarter the better. You are turned on more quickly by a great mind than by a great body. *However*, physical attractiveness is very important to you. You have to be proud of your partner. You are privately very sexy, but you do not show this outwardly. If your new lover is not all that great in bed, you are willing to serve as teacher. Sex is important; you can be a very demanding playmate.

S: For you, it is business before pleasure. If you are in any way bothered by career, business, or money concerns, you find it very hard to relax and get into the mood. You can be romantically idealistic to a fault and are capable of much sensuality. But you never lose control of your emotions. You are very careful and cautious before you give your heart away—and your body, for that matter. Once you make the commitment, though, you stick like glue.

T: You are very sensitive, private, and sexually passive; you like a partner who takes the lead. You get turned on by music, soft lights, and romantic thoughts. You fantasize and tend to fall in and out of love. When in love, you are romantic, idealistic, mushy, and extremely changeable. You enjoy having your senses and your feelings stimulated, titillated, and teased. You are a great flirt. You can make your relationships fit your dreams, all in your own head.

U: You are enthusiastic and idealistic when in love. When not in love, you are in love with love, always looking for someone to adore. You see romance as a challenge. You are a roamer and need adventure, excitement, and freedom. You deal in potential relationships. You enjoy giving gifts and enjoy seeing your mate look good. Your sex drive is strong and you desire instant gratification. You are willing to put your partner's pleasures above your own.

V: You are individualistic and you need freedom, space, and excitement. You wait until you know someone well before committing yourself. Knowing someone means psyching them out. You feel a need to get into their head to see what makes them tick. You are attracted to unusual, eccentric types. Quite often there is an age difference between you and your lover. You respond to danger, thrills, and suspense. The gay scene turns you on, even though you yourself may not be a participant.

W: You are very proud, determined, and you refuse to

take no for an answer when pursuing love. Your ego is at stake. You are romantic, idealistic, and often in love with love itself, not seeing your partner as he or she really is. You feel deeply and throw all of yourself into your relationships. Nothing is too good for your lover. You enjoy playing love games.

X: You need constant stimulation as you are bored quickly. You can handle more than one relationship at a time with ease. You can't shut off your mind. You talk while you make love. You can have the greatest love affairs, all by yourself, in your own head.

Y: You are sexual, sensual, and very independent. If you can't have it your way, you will forgo the whole thing. You want to control your relationships, which doesn't always work out too well. You respond to physical stimulation, enjoy necking and spending hours just touching, feeling, and exploring. However, if you can spend your time more profitably making money, you will give up the pleasures of the flesh for the moment. You need to prove to yourself and your partner what a great lover you are. You want feedback on your performance. You are an open, stimulating, romantic bedmate.

Z: You are very romantic, idealistic, and somehow you believe that to love means to suffer. You wind up serving your mate, or attracting people who have unusual troubles. You see yourself as your lover's savior. You are sincere, passionate, lustful, and dreamy. You can't help falling in love. You fantasize and get turned on by movies and magazines. You do not tell others of this secret life, nor of your sexual. fantasies You are easily aroused sexually.

6

Know Your Child

We've seen how names embody energies that we use throughout life, how our actions and reactions are motivated by these energies. The parent-child relationship offers one of the most valuable applications for our knowledge of name evaluation. And in this case, knowledge *is* power, the power to understand your child and yourself. Knowledge of name meanings can actually be used to promote harmony and understanding between parent and child.

The following are descriptions of your child's thrust letter energies. You can apply the same information to the key letter as well. *In this application, use only the first and last letter of the given name or first name used.*

A: Your child will have a constant need to assert his or her personality. Because this child will be so active and assertive, often displaying both frustration and temper, it is important not to misinterpret this behavior by considering the child belligerent or hostile. This child should be given constructive outlets for his or her super-charged physical and mental energies.

B: Your child can often seem lazy, but this is generally not really the case. This child is uncomfortable with change and therefore is slow to act. Your child has a love of creature comforts, luxuries, and pets, live or stuffed. Taking on responsibilities, handling and saving money early in life, are excellent ways to train this child. He or she has a need for peace and harmony, but can be the first to throw a tantrum if pushed too far.

C: Your child has many interests, gets bored easily, and enjoys doing things with his or her hands. This child often has a short attention span and responds well to training that uses the mind and hands simultaneously. Constant change is required, but not necessarily constant challenge.

CH: Your child is very fixed in his or her ambitions and views. This child has high goals, but wants the help of others in reaching these goals. Your child can be stubborn and opinionated, and shows great intelligence potential but seldom uses it fully until school age. This child is usually very mature for his or her age—age six going on eighty-six.

D: Your child is a devoted little helper. This child enjoys family life and should be included in all family activities. If there are siblings, your **D** child will take on duties and responsibilities for them. A demonstrative show of affection is a must for this child: "Don't tell me you love me, show me."

E: Your child has a need to communicate. The axiom "children should be seen not heard" definitely isn't applicable here. If allowed freedom of expression, this child will grow up to be a gregarious, well-adjusted adult. If punished for talking too much, this child can become introverted. Your child has a vivid imagination; be on guard against misinterpreting this as lying.

F: Here is the class monitor. Your child likes to be boss and take center stage, which means he or she might often act up for the sake of getting attention. Early in life, this child should learn to respect the rights of others and to work along with people, rather than be the overseer. The leadership potential is great.

G: Your child has a tendency to go to extremes, being either very diligent or very lazy. He or she seems so capable that adults often forget that this is still a child. This little person can develop psychosomatic illnesses, particularly when forced to do a disliked chore.

H: Let your first gift to this child be a piggy bank. Your child will enjoy counting money. Your child is success-oriented. If allowed early in life to make decisions and take on responsibility, there is no telling how far up the ladder of success your child can climb.

I: This child says, "I want to be loved. I will do anything to make you love me." If ever a child needed to be stroked, this is the one. Your child is very easily pleased and just as easily hurt. He or she can be a slow learner, but once **I** children learn something, it is theirs forever.

J: Mental and physical activity are a must for the **J** child. Games of coordination will fascinate this child. If encouraged early, this child can excel in sports like gymnastics. If not given physical freedom early, he or she will become an avid mental adventurer. Your child has a thirst for knowledge and a hunger for faraway places.

K: Your child is both physically and mentally regenerative. This child is very private, and this need must be respected early in life. You have to give due respect to your child's rights, property, and opinion; in turn, yours will also be respected. If possible, this child really should have his or her own room, straight from the womb.

L: This child is precocious and loving and needs to be fussed over and encouraged. Loud noises, shouting, quarrels, all disturb his or her equilibrium. Your child enjoys socializing and is companionship-oriented. The boys can be charming and the girls can be coquettish. They need to be liked.

M: Your child is a born parent. He or she likes to be busy and likes to be in charge. This child can be somewhat hyper, but if you recognize his or her need to be active and direct this energy constructively, you will have a happy child and will be a happy parent.

N: Your child is an orderly thinker but a disorganized doer. It is important early in life to encourage this child to see things through to completion. His or her basic dilemma is starting too many things at once and then dropping everything in the confusion. Your child can be a bit shy.

O: Obstinacy and tenacity are either virtues or vices for this child. The more you say no, the more your child says yes. This child can be frustrating to you, for he or she seems to take punishment without flinching. This child must be rewarded for the good and ignored for the bad.

P: This is a peace-loving child who has a temper and a tendency to feel frustrated, moody, and misunderstood. This child requires a constant stream of reassurances and love from his or her parents. There will be pouting in order to receive pampering. Your child has a need to maintain his or her individuality at all costs.

Q: Busy, busy Q. Your child is active, physically as well as mentally, and very tiring for you. He or she should be supplied with a great many toys and distractions to keep head and hands busy.

R: Your child is very bright, but does not fully accept the fact that his or her thoughts are valid. This child deals better on a rational than on an emotional basis. You should try to apply logic and reason in learning experiences.

S: Your child is smart, shrewd, and very status- and money-conscious. He or she will respond to tasks that bring honor and reward. You will find this child more serious than most other children. Offer the **S** child money or recognition and the job will get done.

T: Your child is a dreamer. Music, color, and fantasy are good tools for growth. Your child lives in the world of the mind. If not stifled, the imagination will flower into creative skills. Your child needs to choose his or her own space and private time.

U: Your child will grow to have a humanitarian nature. This child should be involved in games that develop sportsmanship early in life for fair play will have as much appeal as the joy of winning. Your child is a sharer, often to excess. Generosity and kindness are strong character traits.

V: Don't crowd your child in; he or she will often be a loner finding his or her own company as enjoyable as that of others. Your child possesses the ability to grasp new ideas and learn new skills, but may not always do this as quickly as you would expect. This child is very much an individualist who does not usually conform.

W: A strong will coupled with pride makes this child go from one extreme to another, from loyalty and devotion to family, to acting distant and feeling completely misunderstood. Your child can turn adversity into success. His or her determination does not easily allow for failure.

X: Your child is multitalented, quick-thinking, changeable, and hard to keep up with. Now you see him, now you don't. **X** can be in any place at any time, doing anything.

Y: Don't waste your time, parents; this child will get his or her own way anyway. You will often wonder who is the parent and who is the child. In some cases you will never find out. Your child works well on his or her own and thrives on responsibility.

Z: Your child seems to get into everything and has to be taught the meaning of caution early. This child tends to do things the hard way, but can be shown there are easier ways. Your child definitely needs privacy and time alone. He or she learns best through books. Your child will quickly and easily respond to the written word.

7

Finding the Spiritual Lessons in Your Name

Our first recorded name carries as much information about our soul's journey in the world as does the date written on that document. Ancient cultures were well aware of the importance of the name bestowed upon the newly arrived soul on earth. Naming a child was not taken lightly. This respect for names has been carried over into modern culture through naming ceremonies found in the Jewish and Christian faiths. Today, however, most people are not *consciously* aware of the spiritual meanings to be found within the letters of a newborn's name.

Acrophonology comes from the Kabbalah and is based on the teachings of the ancient Hebrew mystics, teachings that address the essentially spiritual nature of man. The Hebrew language is written from right to left. Therefore, we consider the last letter of the original recorded given name (the key letter) to be a spiritual guidepost of prime importance in interpreting the individual's personality. Your spiritual key letter will show the energies that can be employed daily to raise your spiritual consciousness.

The descriptions for the letters listed below will reveal the strengths that can be tapped for your spiritual development. Apply these descriptions to the last letter (key letter) of the original documented given or first name. Also check the description for the last letter of a first name that is currently in use, if it differs from the recorded birth name. These energies can be used as well to give you more information on your spiritual evolution.

One can also build a spiritual composite from all the letters found on one's birth certificate name by examining the descriptions for all the letters therein. However, we consider the key letter to be the most prominent spiritual letter in a name.

A: Your spiritual strength lies in your ability to carry out objective leadership. You can lead for the benefit of others, rather than taking the lead for your own gain. When advancing yourself, you can advance others as well. When fighting for your own rights, you can fight for the rights of others too.

B: Your spiritual strength lies in your ability to place the proper value on money and possessions. You are adept at using, not abusing things of the material world. You know the true value of relationships innately, how to give and receive love and how to deal with people. You respect the needs of others.

C: Your spiritual strength lies in your ability to learn from your environment, to make the proper use of the energies around you, and to be a connector, a link between people. You can bring people together for the mutual benefit of all. You are a disseminator of information.

CH: Your spiritual strength lies in your ability to overcome adversity, rise to new challenges, and be a source of steadiness and support to those around you. You can purge yourself emotionally, thus releasing your gift of love to all.

D: Your spiritual strength lies in your ability to relate beyond your family. You are a part of the human family. You can use your emotions to uplift others. Your ability to nurture can be utilized for the benefit of all those around you.

E: Your spiritual strength lies in your ability to express yourself for the benefit of others as well as for yourself. You are a disseminator of information. Your mental abilities can bring knowledge and enlightenment to everyone, even those who have no direct personal contact with you. Speak out!

F: Your spiritual strength lies in your ability to relate to and befriend the people you meet. You can accept people for who they are. Your *joie de vivre* can light up the lives of those around you. Your desire to love and be loved can go beyond the personal level to the divine within.

G: Your spiritual strength lies in your ability to give wise service, that is, to help where it is most needed. Give service for the sake and joy of giving. When you strive for perfection, strive for God's perfection, not your own. Helping others discriminate helps you.

H: Your spiritual strength lies in your ability to take responsibility for your own actions as well as the actions of others. You *are* your brother's keeper. Your ability to handle business and money matters must be used for the benefit of society, not only for your own gain.

I: Your spiritual strength lies in your ability to give and receive love. It is just as important to let others love you as it is for you to love them. You share, are kind, and give love for love's sake, not for what you can get in return. You know the value of love, wealth, and abundance.

J: Your spiritual strength lies in your sense of justice, your knowledge of right and wrong. You can judge yourself morally. You must learn not to judge others, but accept them for their actions, seeing their divine light within. Your sense of compassion and your desire to make things right wins out.

K: Your spiritual strength lies in your inner fortitude and faith, which can overcome all obstacles to your success. You can set examples for others with your unending ability to bounce back and rise above troubles. You should be a channel for divine power, not your own willpower.

L: Your spiritual strength lies in your ability to bring balance and harmony to all situations. You can use your diplomacy to smooth the way for the benefit of all. Your sense of aesthetics and beauty can enhance your surroundings and bring pleasure to all.

M: Your spiritual strength lies in your ability to make your talents and productivity rise above the level of busywork and really count for something. Be usefully active for the benefit of others, not just yourself. Do not nurture only those close to you, but give help and love to all. Your ties go beyond your personal family.

N: Your spiritual strength lies in your ability to be organized, discriminating, and orderly. These qualities make the service you do for others especially valuable. Your awareness of health matters can be used for others as well as your own benefit. You must give wise service, service for the sake of helping when help is truly needed.

O: Your spiritual strength lies in your ability to see through things, to go beyond surface appearances. You never give up seeking truth or solutions. You refuse to accept defeat, and in doing so, set an example of fortitude and faith for others. You can help others by following your inner feelings.

P: Your spiritual strength lies in your respect for and insight into the value of human dignity. You will always keep your head up high and, in so doing, show others the way. Fairness, justice, and equality are important to you, not only as they concern you yourself, but as they concern others. You champion the underdog.

Q: Your spiritual strength lies in your ability to tell right from wrong and to tell the truth. Your belief in principles sustains you. This allows you to lead the way for others and propagate truth, justice, and spiritual goals in the world.

R: Your spiritual strength lies in your ability to use your sharp mind to make decisions and take actions. You can lead others and put all doubts behind. You can use your knack for positive thinking and your leadership abilities for the advancement of others as well as yourself.

S: Your spiritual strength lies in your ability to guide others. Your actions and the example you set speak for you. Your ability to handle money and business qualifies you to lead others in mundane matters. Your disposition and administration of responsibility allows you to gain the trust and respect of your peers.

T: Your spiritual strength lies in your compassion for your fellow man. You desire to alleviate suffering, to be of service. You must guard against unwise service in your desire to give of yourself. Your sense of humility gives you the privilege to bestow true love, universal love.

U: Your spiritual strength lies in your true sense of giving. When you give, you give from the heart, without strings, seeking nothing in return. You do much for yourself and others. You are blessed and you wish to share your blessings with others. Your mind and heart must always stay open.

V: Your spiritual strength lies in your ability to detach yourself from situations. In doing so, you can render practical aid. And you do not discriminate—you give aid equally to all those who ask. You accept people openly, asking for nothing but their friendship and offering your own in return. You are a humanitarian.

W: Your spiritual strength lies in your sense of universal pride. You can let go of personal pride, personal ego, and take pride in your fellow man. The spiritual sun shining within you can light up the lives of those around you. Your ability to encourage and lead must be used for the benefit of all.

X: Your spiritual strength lies in your ability to go with the flow, remain loose, and not become attached to people, places, and things. Your interaction with your environment is your key to bringing people together for mutual aid and benefit. You are a link in the chain of life.

Y: Your spiritual strength lies in your ability to follow through and have the courage of your convictions, thus setting an example for others. You can take charge and take on responsibility while maintaining your own independence. You are an inspiration to others.

Z: Your spiritual strength lies in your awareness of other realms of reality, in your belief in a reality beyond the physical, and in your ability to receive and give spiritual and inspirational guidance. Your challenge lies in remaining an open channel for higher cosmic forces while keeping a humble attitude.

8

Change Your Name—Change Your Destiny

Changing the name you use can change the energy you use—the energy that flows through you and the energy that you attract. Energy, which, for our purposes, describes the fundamental, universal life force, vibrates and moves at varying rates. We experience it in the form of people, places, and daily events.

Einstein stated that energy returns to its source, moving along a circular path. Whatever energy patterns we send out will return to us, in some form or other. The Bible speaks of this when we read the injunction, "Whatsoever a man soweth, that shall he also reap."

The Bible is, in fact, peppered with stories where name

changes occur with destiny changes. Saul was a man of violence until he changed his name to Paul. After Jacob wrestled with the angel his name was changed to Israel.

The Bible also holds stories in which name changes actually affected one's future. There is the tale of Abram and Sarai. Their marriage was childless, much to their sorrow. Although both were elderly and Sarai well past the years of fruitful bearing, they were told to change their names to create the energies that would beget a child. Abram became Abraham and Sarai became Sarah. Soon after, a son was born to them.

It is a custom among many societies to rename a person during times of grave illness. When a man nears death, a religious leader is consulted, and the ill individual is given a new name in order to receive a revitalized energy flow. From that moment on he is known by the new name. This tradition is still practiced today.

Some Native American peoples make use of name changes when making life changes. New names are taken whenever necessary and as often as necessary, to fit the ever evolving needs of the individual. Among many peoples it is common, upon attaining a spiritual initiation, to take a new name, one that depicts the spiritual goals and forces of nature associated with the initiation. Names relating to air, fire, earth, and water are taken.

It is an astrological belief that your date, time, and place of birth are predestined. We believe that your name is predestined, as well. It is your soul or your consciousness that puts the idea of your name into the minds of your parents. Perhaps it even comes from a higher source.

We can find many references in the Bible that indicate that names are predestined. It is told there that God spoke to Abraham and said, "Sarah thy wife shall bear thee a son indeed; and thou shalt call his name Isaac." And, of course, the classic example of prenatal naming is found in the Angel's message to Mary: "Behold, a virgin shall conceive, and bear a son, and shall call his name Immanuel."

We are told that character changes are a result of changes in our life choices. Inner (psychological) changes do sometimes bring about name changes. Altering our mental and emotional makeup—or energy patterns—will alter our outer expression of self. This will result in life-style changes—changes in the people, places, and events in our daily lives. Thus a change in character and direction will naturally be reflected in our name. We can no longer respond to the old vibrations.

There are two schools of thought on altering destiny. One states that only an inner change can result in a change in life circumstances. The other maintains that basic personal revision can also be worked from the outside in. A change in the physical or outer patterns—like changing one's name—can alter the inner mechanisms of the psyche, and thereby change one's choices, goals, and path. This is the school of thought to which we adhere, because we've seen that name changes *do* bring about life changes. Or, conversely, a change in goals can be marked by a change in name.

We all have many potentials that we do not utilize. . . . We are all multifaceted. All of our possible life paths are indicated in the name we receive at birth; in essence, that name holds our destiny. Our free will allows us to pick and choose the energies we want to work with—those character traits, latent talents, and abilities we desire to develop. There is a big difference between destiny and free will! The name recorded at birth embodies destiny. Additional names offer choices and the opportunity to exercise our own free will.

A new personality projection is available through name modifications. For example, a person whose name ends in the letter Y (a Mary, for instance) prefers doing things her own way. But if the same person changes her name to Marie this may no longer be the case. The difference between Mary and Marie is that Marie will readily discuss problems and be more open to change.

A name change indicates conscious growth, for *you are adding energies, never deleting them*. The influences of a name not currently in use become subliminal, while the energies of the new name are projected and become apparent. The results of alterations in spelling and/or letter arrangements in a name, as well as a full or partial name change, take effect approximately six months after a name modification. The qualities of the old name diminish within six months to one year.

An example of a name change is that of Norma Jean Baker, who changed her name to Marilyn Monroe.

NORMA

The **N** thrust letter shows a personality of self-criticism and a striving for perfection. The **O** shows a tendency toward compulsive behavior. It depicts an intense individual who can put all of herself into one area. The **R** is a hinge letter, which shows she was insecure about her intellect. She married playwright Arthur Miller partly to help fulfill her intellectual needs. **M** suggests close ties to family and friends, and a tendency to worry and emotional overreacting. The key letter **A** shows a need to conclude things through independent action and to never look back.

JEAN

The **J** thrust letter speaks of a love of sports, travel, and adventure. She married the famous baseball player Joe DiMaggio. The **J** thrust letter also indicates close relationships that tend to be with individuals who are interesting, diversified, and talkative. **E** indicates that she was clever, witty, and inventive, as well as nervous, restless, and a sometimes scattered thinker. **A** signals a strong desire to be active both mentally and physically. It also shows that she wanted her independence and had a strong desire to be her own person. The **N** key shows she could be exacting, meticulous, and mentally compartmentalized.

BAKER

B as a first surname letter indicates an aptitude for a career that deals in financial matters as well as luxury items. It tells us she was willing to work hard so that she would not have to work. The **A** energy here is a repeat of the **A** energy found in Jean. The **K** hinge letter shows that she had a compulsion for change and rebirth in all areas of her life. She may also have felt a need to guard her health. **E** demonstrates the same energy as the **E** in Jean. The **R** key letter tells us that she tended to wrap things up by taking actions only after careful consideration.

When she took on her new stage name, these personality traits, though still there, were pushed into the background of her life, and new ones began to dominate.

MARILYN

As Marilyn, she projected the following qualities: **M** as her thrust letter showed her to be a very active, busy person, with a need to feel productive and useful. Her feelings and sensitivities ran silent and deep. She had a tendency to be hyper, to overreact and worry excessively. Family ties became a major part of her life. These qualities were already indicated by the **M** in her birth name, Norma; however, as the **M** was not a thrust or key letter, it was not as strongly emphasized or as frequently used in her daily life. The **A** is the same energy as **A** in Jean or Baker. The **R** is the same as in Norma. The **I** hinge letter tells us she had a strong need to give and receive love for love's sake, and a need to be assured of affection. **L** signals that she was social and needed contact with people. **Y** indicates that she sought out positions of authority, responsibility, status, and ways of achieving monetary success, *all in an attempt to overcome deep feelings of insecurity*. The **N** key letter shows a need to be in control. This is the same energy as in Norma, noted by the **N** thrust letter and **N** key letter of Jean.

MONROE

The **M** first letter of a surname hints that she would be happy dealing with the public. **O** is the same random letter as found in Norma. The **N** random letter tells us that she could easily burden herself with guilt. She was quite discerning, discriminating, and shy, even though she enjoyed talking and socializing. The **R** and **O** random letters are the same as in Norma. The **E** key letter indicates that she was a talker, who, nevertheless, may not always have expressed herself fully.

Points to Consider When Changing Your Name

If you wish to change your name, first define your goals. What do you expect from the change? What do you hope to accomplish? Do you wish to make a career change?

Do you hope to enhance your personality expression? Do you want to eliminate an unwanted character trait? Go through the dictionary section of this book to pick out the letter whose definition best illustrates your desired results.

THRUST LETTER: This is the strongest energy expressor to be found in a name.

KEY LETTER: This letter is the next strongest position for energy expression and use.

FIRST LETTER OF SURNAME: This position aids in career as well as personality expression. Thrust letters and key letters are just as powerful in career concerns as well. Work choices and character traits can never be entirely separated.

RANDOM LETTER: This is an even and constant energy flow.

HINGE LETTER: A name containing a hinge letter should be avoided. Hinge letters suggest blocked energy flow, thus holding the possibility of problems and difficulties in the areas of life with which the letter deals. *However, hinge letters can bring challenges as well, which, when met, provide strength and positive momentum in life.*

DOUBLE LETTERS: A single name containing double letters should be avoided. Double letters pack a double whammy of an energy flow, which can sometimes become too much of a good thing. They can prove to be an exaggeration of the qualities expressed by the letter.

MULTIPLE LETTERS: A single or full name containing three or more of one letter should be avoided, if possible, for the same reasons as above in the double letter category.

The following is a sampling of traits that are fostered by usage of the letters listed. (This is not a complete list.)

Assertiveness: A, F, J, R
Intellectualism: C, E, L, P, R
Expressiveness, Verbalization: E, J, N, P
Business Orientation: B, H, N, S, Y
Health, Service Work: G, N, T
Artistic ability, Creativity: B, I, J, L, T
Nurturant: D, M, O

We don't advise that you attempt to change your name until you've read and digested this entire book. Name changing is serious business, and any ill-advised moves could actually prove harmful to your personality. You can't go about it on a hypothetical basis. You first must learn who you are and what you want out of life. This book is designed to help you do just that by giving you greater insight into yourself, as well as into those you love and deal with. It can help you expand your capabilities. It can help you take charge of your life!

James Greene and David Lewis

The Hidden Language of Your Handwriting £1.95

Explore the personalities, passions and problems of those about you with just a few lines of their handwriting and this fascinating book. Check out your new employee – or your new boss – understand your children better – learn the deep sexual need of your partner – spot the early warnings of illness. *The Hidden Language of Your Handwriting* is the first non-technical guide to the new science of graphonomy – an exact and perceptive method of decoding the handwritten word.

Leonard Cataldo and Robert Pelletier

Be Your Own Astrologer £3.95

Construct your own birth chart in under twenty minutes. Discover what the stars reveal . . . Two professional astrologers open up the world of astrology to everyone wanting to find the key to their unique personality. Armed just with your birthdate you can construct a simple profile. Or, to delve deeper, here's how to complete a complex chart, in fascinating detail.

Maurice Mességué

Health Secrets or Plants and Herbs £2.50

Man has been aware of the medicinal powers of plant life since the dawn of civilization. In this unique reference book, the famous herbalist Maurice Mességué describes the therapeutic properties of a hundred different species of plants and herbs, how to grow them and how to prepare the balms, lotions, infusions and ointments that will bring natural healing.

Linda Goodman
Linda Goodman's Sun Signs £2.95

Have you ever wondered about yourself? What you are really like, whether you'll make a good wife, mother or lover, whether other people like you? Linda Goodman reveals the real you, your personality and character as the stars see you, in this remarkably lively and down-to-earth book.

Linda Goodman's Love Signs £3.95

A new approach to the human heart and personal relationships. A compulsively readable book exploring the tensions and harmony inherent in your associations with people born under the same sun sign as yourself, or under the other eleven signs. Also features: in-depth exploration of the seventy-eight sun sign patterns for both sexes; lists of famous people under your sign; explanations of the twelve mysteries of love.

Teri King
Love, Sex and Astrology £1.75

Revealing advice for would-be lovers. Spot your ideal partner; know the mating possibilities of the zodiac; find the strengths and weaknesses of your sign – through penetrating questionnaires. Teri King answers many questions on love, sex, careers and children with humour, wit and a deal of common sense.

'All quite irresistible' MANCHESTER EVENING NEWS

Julius Fast

Body Language £1.75

Every move you make reveals a secret . . . This important book adds a new dimension to human understanding. Julius Fast teaches how to penetrate the personal secrets of strangers, friends and lovers by interpreting their body movements – and how to make use of the power thus gained.

Francis Hitching

The World Atlas of Mysteries £6.95

From the origins of the universe and terrestrial life, through the unique development of man, to the secrets of ancient civilizations and bizarre phenomena in the sky and beyond – the enormous scope of this encyclopedia, its exhaustive research and copious illustrations (maps, photographs, diagrams) make it a unique and fascinating book. Francis Hitching, author of *Earth Magic,* is one of the world's leading authorities on the inexplicable and the unexplained.

'A book of absorbing interest to anyone who believes that there are more things in heaven and earth than science will recognize' DR KIT PEDLER, EVENING NEWS

Jean-Charles de Fontbrune

Nostradamus: Countdown to Apocalypse £2.50

He worked alone, a man versed in the secret writings, a historian of the future who generations have recognised as the greatest seer Europe has ever known. The rise of Napoleon, the Bolshevik revolution, two world wars, the sudden wealth of Arab power, the attempted assassination of a pope from Poland. And the chronology of the apocalypse. A Soviet invasion of Britain in the 1990s, the destruction of the House of Commons, nuclear holocaust in 1999, the year of the apocalypse . . .